FULL CIRCLE

youth ministry
that begins and
ends with
Jesus

by

Charlie Alcock

wesleyan
PUBLISHING HOUSE
wphstore.com
Fishers, IN

Published by Wesleyan Publishing House, Fishers, Indiana 46037
www.wesleyan.org/wph
Printed in the United States of America
ISBN: 978-1-63257-576-0
ISBN (e-book): 978-1-63257-577-7

CONTENTS

PREFACE

AS A KID, I DISTINCTLY remember the first time I ever went to the county fair. The first thing I did was run to where all the rides were. There was one shaped like a pirate ship. Now, the pirate ship is a pendulum-type ride that swings back and forth until you feel like it's going to flip over. I didn't understand this as a kid; I just wanted to jump on. And jump on I did until I was so sick I could not wait to get off that ride. From that point on in my life, I would try to avoid any ride that looked like a pendulum whether it was at the state fair or a major theme park. My first experience on that giant pendulum was enough for me for a lifetime.

This is the way I have felt about most of my ministry experience. It seems like we're on this giant pendulum swing that's going back and forth and the moment that you feel like you have a handle on what you're doing or what's next, there is a sudden change of direction. I would feel like things were going well and without warning ministry trends start swinging back the other way. In a way I've been ministry sick for many years because the pendulum simply never stops. For most of my ministry life it made me feel guilty and even inadequate. I wasn't measuring up to what others were doing or what other ministries looked like. This led to me chasing the next big thing and not chasing what I really needed to see as my model: my Leader. I understood that Jesus was the way, the truth, and the life, but after that, what's next? It took me a while in ministry to see that not only was Jesus the life-giving force in a person's life—the center of ministry—but also an incredible leader of people in day-to-day ministry. Is it possible that Jesus modeled for us a way to do ministry day-to-day?

It's time to get off that crazy pendulum ride. Here is a warning: the pendulum will never stop swinging on its own. The big question I want to address is this: how do we stop the back-and-forth swinging? What I've realized is, we've set our sights on models of ministry rather than the Author of the movement. We are all trying to figure out how to make disciples and the best way to align ourselves with the community we serve. We all want to maximize our resources and develop programs that will help us do more of what we need to do. We all have hopes and dreams and, may I suggest, visions that God has given us for the community we serve. We all know that with Jesus all things are possible. I don't question the motives of people I have served with or even of those in the ministry across town that I have only heard about. I think we all want to do the same exact thing: we want the name of Jesus to be made known.

Let's take a little journey and look beyond a model that we have seen in another ministry or even one that we ourselves have crafted. Can we step into a new way of doing ministry, one that looks specifically at Jesus and how he did ministry? I want to ask this question…if it matters to Jesus and it's how he ministered, why would we do anything else?

My hope is to provide some practical truths to help discern and discover how God is moving in our specific context where we minister and, at the same time, unify us as people committed to ministry. I also hope that this book rekindles a fire in you—to do ministry that results in life change. This book isn't solely focused on details about doing ministry, but rather, why we do ministry and how we follow Jesus' way of doing ministry. I want this book to rekindle your passion to embrace a movement over a specific model.

I didn't like those pendulum rides as a kid and I like them less after all these years of ministry when I see how it makes the church sick. The back and forth needs to change to a forward-motion approach to ministry that is based on one model, one person—and his name is Jesus.

ACKNOWLEDGMENTS

I WANT TO SAY THANK you to the students whom I have had the privilege of pastoring. It's the lessons you've taught me that are expressed here. It's the youth groups meeting every week—the camps, retreats, missions trips, and bus rides all over the country—that have forged relationships that have bonded us together for a lifetime. At the center of it all is Christ, and that's why we still tell stories and share memories. I'm continually reminded of you as I keep mementos of our adventures on my office shelves, drive past certain buildings, see a social media post from you, attend a wedding, or eat some carne asada.

I want to thank all the contributors who jumped in to help write the "Think Practical" section. Your voice, your ministry experience, and your willingness to invest in people will bless all who read this resource and help them along their ministry journey. I want to thank Sharie Schnell for catching the vision of this book and crafting the visual component that captures the vision.

I want to thank my family. Joy, Nathaniel, Nicholas, and Emily have lived this. How many times were we at a summer camp with three kids? How many discipleship groups did Joy lead with Emily in a stroller? At how many camps were Nathaniel and Nicholas the team mascots or featured in the camp highlight video? I want to say a special thanks to Nicholas for walking with me as the first reader of this resource and doing so much editing before it was ever turned in. More than proofreading, you understood me and why this book was so important to me.

THINK BIBLICAL

FULL CIRCLE

THINK BIBLICAL

I HAVE ALWAYS LOVED TO build things. As a little kid, I would rather build a toy than buy one. I would build forts out of snow or leftover barn wood that were big enough to walk through, and my favorite toy inside the house was Lincoln Logs. The desire to craft and build things would later become a creative element of my ministry, and one that I still embrace today.

Because of this design side of my brain, I have had opportunities to work with churches that wanted to reimagine their spaces for students. One church was located just outside of Indianapolis. My task was to walk beside the youth ministry team and reimagine their program and ministry space. The team wanted to hear from people who were deeply invested in the ministry and called this church home. One person I met with was a leader in the community with ties to college athletics. I was new to this church and didn't personally know him, but quickly learned about his work. In a meeting one day, I found myself hanging on to his every word; I loved everything he shared. It was late in the meeting when he explained something so basic yet so incredibly profound. He explained how an organization could be unified if everyone could simply agree on why we do what we do. He talked about his task of doing this very thing when it came to college athletics. In the professional world of the NCAA, his goal was to get everyone to agree on why college athletics exist. He unpacked a principle that applies to all sports regardless of what they are, where they are played, or who participates: college athletics are about the athlete first and foremost. The college athlete is the *why*. He elaborated that if everyone could agree on that, then the rest—the *what, when, where,* and *how*—could be organized to ensure a level playing field for all.

During the breaks, I wouldn't let him eat his lunch because of all the questions I was slinging his way. Near the end of our conversation, he restated that if college athletics were in agreement on strategy, then they could have a common platform and figure out how to work with each other for the sake of the student athlete as well as the sport they participated in. The *why* was the strategy, and the rest were just tactics.

I shifted from college sports and started thinking about how the church needs to be unified with the same strategy. I began asking pastors and leaders from diverse ministries in the United States and abroad if they could define their strategies. Every answer I received was different, leading me to see ministry from multiple different perspectives. I know we are all on the same page when it comes to Jesus as Lord and Savior. I know we all desire to see life change in people around us as well as in our own lives, yet I was seeing a massive breakdown in how we talk about ministry with each other and how incredibly confusing it is to people both in the church and outside of it. I saw a need to get back to the basics and for pastors and leaders to get on the same page. We need to do this for the sake of all the people we care about. People don't understand why different churches focus on such different aspects of the Christian faith or why they care so much about some things and so little about others. Why does one church focus on Jesus as the great evangelist who loved lost people—the shepherd who would leave the flock to rescue lost sheep? Why does the church down the street only talk about the Jesus who did miracles and preached to the multitudes? Why does another church only focus on small groups, and everything else is considered a waste of time? Can't we all have the same strategy while being diverse in our tactics? It's time for leaders to get unified around Jesus' strategy, for the sake of the churched and the unchurched.

IF IT MATTERS TO JESUS, IT MATTERS TO ME

One of the greatest opportunities I've ever had in ministry was studying the Synoptic Gospels with Dr. Kenneth Waters at a university in downtown Los Angeles. During our course together, we unpacked these accounts of Jesus' life and the ways Jesus modeled leadership for his followers. I had long considered Jesus as simply the object of ministry, but as we got deeper into Scripture, I started to uncover a major blind spot. The Synoptic Gospels show us that Jesus is not only the object of our ministry, but the author of how to do ministry. I began comparing how I'd been conducting my ministry with what I found in the Gospels, and the results horrified me. I had been doing ministry the way I saw fit, the way I thought it should be done. My strategies for worship and discipleship were based more on what I saw my peers doing than on what was perfectly laid out by Jesus. By overlaying my design of ministry with that of Jesus, I knew that I had to go back to square one.

I felt two drastically different emotions during this time. One was incredible excitement that comes with new discovery. The other was shame and embarrassment. I had always known Jesus as Savior, but I never really looked at him in the context of leading and shepherding people. It was always Jesus as my personal example, not Jesus as my model for leadership. How could I miss this aspect that's so ingrained in his ministry? My limited and localized view had gotten in the way and, like many of us do, I had let that small perspective carry too much weight.

As leaders we often turn our attention on ourselves and how we are individually built for ministry. We focus on how ministry works for us specifically rather than how we fit in Jesus' ministry more broadly. We let our specific strengths dictate our agendas, relying on them to distinguish us from other ministries. We all have unique gifts and talents, but who is the author of those? If we are all on the same team and under the same direction of Jesus, when did our own gifts and talents become what defines our ministry? When did the focus go from what unifies us to what makes us different from each other? We often rely on our own knowledge and abilities, and Jesus is our backup plan.

Let's be crystal clear: our gifts and talents are given to us, and our responsibility is to steward them. They are what we offer back to Jesus and his church, the body of Christ. Yet they don't define us. Those same gifts and talents can drag our gaze away from the example Jesus set forth. The danger here is that they can cause us to become myopic in the way we structure ministry in our communities.

As Dr. Waters guided the course on the Synoptic Gospels, my eyes were opened to how Jesus did ministry with so many different people throughout distinct seasons of his life. In addition to the disciples and his growing group of followers, Jesus was invested in a wide range of people. From those who simply noticed him to those who talked negatively about him—or who were unsure of him and didn't trust him—he took the time to invest in anyone who wanted to know him more. As he discipled those walking with him, those he worshiped with and broke bread with, he desired to see others added to their number. He modeled a commitment to a core ministry team and, at the same time, modeled a commitment to connecting with and reaching everyone.

Looking back, I realize one of the best things Dr. Waters taught me was that our ministry is not supported by Scripture; rather, Scripture is what defines our ministry. I think I always believed this, I just never really put it into words.

In a conversation with Dr. Dave Smith, a dear friend of mine and New Testament scholar, he reminded me that our ministry literally flows from the very voice of Jesus (the Latin expression is *Ipsissima Vox* meaning "the very voice"). In this conversation, Dave also pointed out that the disciples were much like a group of young students attending their first day of class in college. There was so much to learn and Jesus did something that we must do today: he walked with them instead of just telling them what direction to go. Jesus made himself known to people, those who would follow him and those who just came to hear him talk.

At the 30,000-foot perspective, we can see how Jesus was doing all this with such grace and skill. Those he ministered to weren't fully aware of who he was or the significance of his ministry; it was all happening before he went to the cross, defeating sin and death. For his disciples, Jesus was demonstrating how they should carry out his ministry on their own, showing how they could utilize their gifts and talents to realize their purpose, edify the body, and unify believers. Nearing the cross, Jesus leaned into his disciples, challenging the strength of their faith and intensifying the significance of his message for them. In short, he was investing his legacy in both a core group and the community more broadly. What's amazing to me is how Jesus did all of this at the same time! Jesus could invest in a relationship with someone who didn't even know or trust him, and at the same time be in a deep relationship with someone who had committed their whole life to follow him.

A story that illustrated the significance of this concurrent commitment is the feeding of the 5,000. Along with the resurrection of Jesus, it's the only miracle recorded in all four of the gospels, and in all four gospels the 30,000-foot perspective is the same. In the story, Jesus had just finished another big ministry moment—the Sermon on the Mount. Those who had heard his message, had been healed, or were just curious, were pressing in and wanting more from him. His ministry team got him in a boat and they headed to the town of Capernaum when word came that John the Baptist, who many believed might be a messiah, had been killed. Imagine for a moment how this news would have affected Jesus. John was not just another acquaintance, he was a beloved friend; the one who leapt in his mother's womb at the sound of Jesus' name, deflected all attention and credit to Jesus as the true Messiah, and baptized him in the Jordan River. In the midst of his grief for John, tired and physically spent from his sermon, Jesus knew that he must continue with the disciples. As they reached the top of the Sea of Galilee near Caperna`um, the crowds followed and more people continued to join them.

Tradition and biblical scholarship help us understand that the count of 5,000 people recorded in Scripture excludes women and children. We're talking about a much larger crowd gathered together, possibly around 18,000, which would have completely overwhelmed the resources of the small town of Capernaum. Also, these people were traveling in the local climate conditions. It's a dry climate, so carrying water and food is essential. (I've walked to this location and stood on the very spot of this amazing miracle before. It's hot!) What did Jesus do when he got out of the boat and saw this huge crowd?

The apostles returned to Jesus and told him all that they had done and taught. And he said to them, "Come away by yourselves to a desolate place and rest a while." For many were coming and going, and they had no leisure even to eat. And they went away in the boat to a desolate place by themselves. Now many saw them going and recognized them, and they ran there on foot from all the towns and got there ahead of them. When he went ashore he saw a great crowd, and he had compassion on them, because they were like sheep without a shepherd. And he began to teach them many things. (Mark 6:30–34 ESV)

Jesus had compassion. This large group had been captivated by his teaching and awed by his miracles. They were hoping he might be the Messiah and were following him around the region trying to catch more of what he might say or do. What about those who were being discipled by Jesus? What did they want to do?

By this time it was late in the day, so his disciples came to him. "This is a remote place," they said, "and it's already very late. Send the people away so that they can go to the surrounding countryside and villages and buy themselves something to eat." But he answered, "You give them something to eat" (Mark 6:35–37).

Jesus asked one of the disciples, Philip, how the people could be fed. Not only did Philip learn a lesson of faith, but all of the disciples learned that true faith must rely on divine resources, not physical and material ones. Philip began to tally all of the meager supplies the disciples had among them, and somewhat stymied, said, "Shall we go and buy two hundred pennyworth worth of bread, and give them to eat?" (Mark 6:37 KJV). One pennyworth was a day's wage at the time. In John 6:9, Andrew brings a young boy to Jesus and says, "Here is a boy with five small barley loaves and two small fish, but how far will they go among so many?" The boy could have refused to give up his lunch. He could have chosen to run away when the disciple approached him and asked if he would sacrifice his meal for Jesus. Neither Andrew nor the boy knew what Jesus would do, but this boy allowed Jesus to use his little gift. He trusted Christ with his possessions without knowing what the outcome would be. What did Jesus do? What did Jesus ask of those who were with him, those who were being developed and trained, those who were closest to him?

He commanded them all to sit down in on the grassin groups, by hundreds and by fifties. And taking the five loaves and the two fish, he looked up to heaven and said a blessing and broke the loaves and gave them to the disciples to set before the people. And he divided the two fish among them all. And they all ate and were satisfied. And they took up twelve baskets full of broken pieces and fish (Mark 6:39–43 ESV).

Clearly there is so much happening here. For much of my life, I only focused on the miracle of the five loaves and two fish. Yet from the 30,000-foot level, the example set forth in Jesus' ministry at this moment is equally amazing. Everyone was fed and ministered to. His community of followers were there and witnessed it all. They worshiped him in these moments. Those being discipled by Jesus were challenged by his actions and words. They began to understand his message and, even more, his identity as the coming Messiah.

Those who were closest to Jesus were challenged and rebuked for their lack of concern for the people. The disciples asked Jesus to send the crowd away, and yet Jesus included them in the miracle. The disciples had to put their faith into action and carry those twelve baskets of food. Can you imagine having a basket of food and facing thousands of people with it? I would have been scared of running out of food or being torn to pieces by an angry crowd. That didn't happen. Can you imagine what it would have felt like to carry the basket and see everyone fed? That would be a life-changing moment.

I clearly see Jesus with a deep concern and love for all those who need him but have not yet accepted him. I see Jesus in community with those who are following him. I see Jesus discipling and challenging those who know him best by including them in the process and challenging them to become leaders in that process. They can't just observe; they must put their faith into action. Jesus shows us that he is an amazing leader by focusing on all of these areas simultaneously.

Remember earlier when I was talking about gifts and talents? Some of you are gifted and have a special place in your heart for the moments in Jesus' ministry when he connected with people who are much like you. Jesus connected with people who are just like you today. People were on their own spiritual journey and, like you, had a desire to lead and influence others and discover their purpose and place. You are drawn to those people who are like you, and your unique set of gifts only accents this. Good for you! However, you must remember everything we just talked about and keep that 30,000-foot perspective. Your tendency is going to lead you to really focus in, encouraging others to join you in making this the primary goal of your ministry. However, that is not what Jesus did and not how we should proceed. The primary goal of your ministry is to reflect and mimic the ministry of Jesus in all areas, focusing on them simultaneously as Jesus did.

Here is how I understand the ministry of Jesus broken down into five areas that may help you as you design and implement ministry in the place you are. This is not a deep dive, but a more basic overview help to get a better perspective. Remember, this is not a linear model or chart. Jesus did all of these simultaneously.

THE GOAL

Everything we do centers around one goal: making lifelong disciples who think and act like Jesus. Being a disciple begins the moment you enter into a relationship with Jesus. The very moment you ask Jesus to forgive you and receive him as Savior, you are a child of God and follower of Jesus. At that very moment you can share what Jesus did for you with others (Everyone) so that they may know him as well. At that very moment you can engage in worship (Worship and Word) as well as join others who make up the body of believers in praise and thanksgiving. At that very moment you can begin growing in your understanding and knowledge, allowing the Holy Spirit to change your heart (Character) and become accountable to others. At that very moment your gifts and talents (Leadership) can be tuned to Jesus' frequency and used to move his kingdom forward.

From the moment you enter into a relationship with Jesus the rest of your life is a discipleship process. How long does it take? Can I take a class and get a certificate in being a disciple of Jesus? Do I need a degree first? What age can I qualify to be a full disciple? If I fail and make a mistake, do I go back to the beginning and start over? All are legitimate questions with no easy answers. Some people experience a total transformation of their heart in an instant: the things they say and do sound and look like Jesus, because they flow from a completely changed heart. For other people, it's a slower process of growing in their faith and understanding; their growth is steady and constant. For me, I failed right out of the gate.

I accepted Jesus as my Savior; I asked him to save me from everything that scared me. I wanted to know Jesus and I knew what I was doing. For me, it was real, but I just couldn't seem to make it work. I was on a spiritual roller-coaster, and I kept failing and then coming back asking Jesus to save me again. It took me years to understand the difference between accepting Jesus as Savior and knowing him as Lord of my life. It's a lifelong commitment that can come with a heavy price. What happened to Peter? Did he retire with his family at his side? No. He was crucified with his family at his side. Surrendering to Jesus as Lord is to come full circle in your relationship with and commitment to Christ, such that you can't help but tell others about him. It becomes your heart's desire to let everyone know what God has done for you and what he can do for them. In following Jesus, you become accountable in relationships, experiencing transparency as together you practice living his way. As a disciple, you offer your gifts and talents for his use, purpose, and glory. You want to follow in his footsteps and reach everyone, worship in community, help others grow more like him, lead by example, and then do it all over again.

After feeding the 5,000, the disciples got back into their boat, and Jesus instructed them to go ahead without him. You know the story. The storm came up, the disciples were scared, and then they saw Jesus walking on the water toward the boat. What did Peter do? He stepped out and literally walked on water until he remembered who he was, took his eyes off Jesus, and looked at his surroundings. I can't blame him or criticize him too much because I have done the very same thing. No, I wasn't walking on water, but I have taken my eyes off Jesus and focused on all the stuff happening around me.

Peter's experience on the water was a turning point in his relationship with Jesus and the other disciples who didn't step out and risk everything. Let's just think about that for a moment. Why did no one else step out of the boat? Peter, as we all know, didn't follow Jesus without more failures. He is remembered every Easter weekend as the one who failed Jesus in epic fashion by denying him three times. But his story doesn't end there. His story is one of redemption and restoration—it's more epic than his failures! Jesus calls Peter the rock on which he will build his church.

It wasn't difficult to see that David was gifted. He could talk to anyone, build anything, fix what was broken, and inspire everyone around him. I got to see his ministry from the beginning—before everyone knew him as Pastor Kujo (that's short for Kujawa). It was as if I was a silent observer—watching this older teenager, like a kid mesmerized by a new toy. And then he saw me. I didn't belong in that group of teens. I was in middle school and they were the cool high school guys. Over time, I got to hang out with them at our church youth ministry gatherings and, if I was lucky, got to ride home in David's car. And let me tell you, he always had a great car.

As time passed and I moved up in high school, David would come to my football games with some other students and cheer me on. Always supportive. Always encouraging. Always pushing me to believe in what

God could do in my life. Honestly, he saw more in me than I saw in myself. After a few years in college and away from home, I got a call from David to meet over break. He had graduated with a business degree but felt God calling him into ministry as a pastor. Just like that, this superhero in my world was going to be my roommate. It was amazing! We prayed together, took classes, studied (yes, we studied), and owned the foosball table at the student center. What I remember the most, however, are all of the late-night conversations we had about ministry. Would God use us? Could God use us? It was safe to dream with David, and I could be vulnerable with him. He was discipling me.

I remember standing up at David's wedding. We were all so proud as this hero of ours was getting married to Marlene, another superhero from our small church. Back in the day, nobody saw that coming. Later, he stood up at my wedding. It was so cool.

At one point, we were both youth pastors in the same town! We did ministry together, planned events together, and, when those were over, we cleaned up together. This became a pattern for us over the next twenty-five years, even when ministry sent us in different directions. It didn't matter if I was in San Diego and he was in Ohio; we figured out how to do ministry together. David was using his gifts and talents to build the kingdom of God and I saw it firsthand.

Not long ago, I had a major decision to make. I called David. That was not uncommon because with every major decision I made I called David. His words were clear and kind. He challenged me to trust the One who had called me. He would call back, follow up with me, and ask me questions that I had to answer truthfully (and yes, he could tell if I didn't). I remember crying with him when my mom died, when my sister died, and he supported me when I had to walk the same road again with my brother. He celebrated with me in the good times, encouraged me in the bad times, and was there to support me in the really hard times. When the news came about his tumor, I really didn't care about what was on the schedule that day. I just drove four hours to the hospital where he was at. Over the next year, all these memories came back like a flood as I recalled the times when I attempted to encourage him, yet he was the one encouraging me back. I think it was during the time that I was preparing for his funeral that I fully realized that David was truly a disciple of Christ.

In John 15, Jesus is teaching about his relationship with the Father and with us. He is the vine, and his Father is the gardener. He is willing to be pruned so that he can grow. Jesus then turns his focus on us when he says he is the vine and we are the branches, and we must be pruned if we are to grow. But the promise is clear: "I am the vine; you are the branches. Whoever abides in me and I in him, he it is that bears much fruit, for apart from me you can do nothing" (John 15:5 ESV).

We must remain in him, and that is a lifetime commitment. The lesson doesn't end there. The more you read, the more intense it gets. If we keep going, we see something that David saw—and in turn helped me to see. In John 15:15, Jesus says, "I no longer call you servants, because a servant does not know his master's business. Instead, I have called you friends, for everything that I learned from my Father I have made known to you."

Jesus doesn't want us to just follow because we fear him or feel like we owe him something for what he has done for us. He wants us to learn from him, know his heart, and grow!

What I have learned over the years is that we can obtain all kinds of information and download all kinds of facts, thinking we know what's really going on. You know the greatest invention in human history is the smartphone. At one point it was the wheel, then it was the Gutenberg printing press. Now we can download information in seconds and have access to almost as much information as the local library. But what I have learned comes from John 15:15, and it was lived out by my dear friend David, is that true understanding only comes through suffering. Think about this question: What lessons have you learned in your life and how did you learn them? You probably learned far more from your mistakes, failures, and the difficulties you faced than from your successes or times when everything seemed easy. A disciple is someone who understands what Jesus is saying here in John 15:15. A disciple wants to understand the Father's heart, know the Father's will, and walk in that relationship for a lifetime.

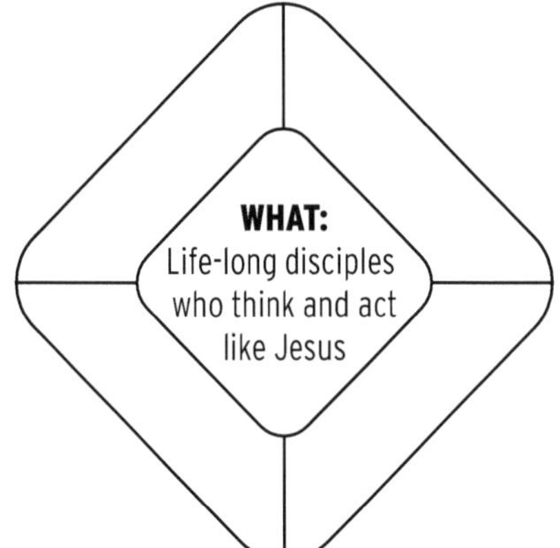

If being a disciple matters to Jesus, being a disciple matters to me.

"WHO" IS EVERYONE?

My understanding of Scripture makes it clear to me that all have sinned and come short of the glory of God: "But now the righteousness of God has been manifested apart from the law, although the Law and the Prophets bear witness to it—the righteousness of God through faith in Jesus Christ for all who believe. For there is no distinction: for all have sinned and fall short of the glory of God" (Rom. 3:21–23 ESV).

Talk about a level playing field for every human ever born! We are all in need of a Savior, and therefore everyone that we come into contact with (and those we don't) needs one as well. The term everyone here is simple and straightforward. All of us who know Jesus as Savior and Lord were at one point in need of his saving grace.

Years ago, I led a mission trip with a group of high school students who were growing in their personal relationship with Jesus. This trip challenged the students as we did ministry with people who did not share the same beliefs or experiences. It was eye opening, hard, and discouraging. Then the trip became amazing. One night we joined a ministry created to reach women in need, including women who were pregnant, homeless, addicted to drugs or alcohol, lonely, hurting, and even some who were escaping prostitution and sex trafficking. Given all of this hurt and pain, what were we going to say? What were we going to do? We thought we were only going to help serve dinner, clean the kitchen, paint some areas of the building, and pray with the leadership there. However, that's not all the leader of this ministry asked for. Just before the evening service, she asked if I would give a word of encouragement and for someone in our group to give a testimony. Our entire group was listening to these instructions but there were no volunteers. As we headed into the room where the service was being held (the same room that would be transformed into a dining hall later) I approached one of our students that I'll call Amy. You should have seen the look on her face! She knew before I even opened my mouth what I was going to ask. She responded, "What am I going to say? I've never done drugs or any of the things these women have done. I have a great family who loves me, and both of my parents are Christian. I have a pretty easy life compared to all of them." I said, "You don't have to compare yourself to them. What do you have in common with them?" After a brief moment of silence between us, I blurted out, "All have sinned and come short of the glory of God. Yes, you were born in a relatively small town to loving and godly parents. Yes, you go to a Christian school and haven't done a bunch of 'bad' things. But tell them the truth. Before you accepted Jesus as your personal Savior you were lost in the same way many of them are lost. Tell them that nothing can separate us from the love of God and that they can find that out just as you have. That is your common ground!" Amy got up during that service and, just like the disciples who were charged with carrying a basket of food to thousands of people, shared a simple yet profound truth. Everyone needs a Savior, and everyone must accept Jesus for themselves. Before Amy asked Jesus into her life, she was one of the people in the crowd listening to Jesus. It didn't matter what "bad" things she had or hadn't done. It didn't matter who her parents were or that she grew up in church. She was lost, and when she asked Jesus into her life, she was found! You should have heard the roar from the group who gathered that night. Amy could hardly finish her last sentence. The whole room affirmed her story and her bravery in telling it. We are all part of the everyone who needs a Savior.

Scripture is clear that Jesus cares about everyone and desires to know them personally:

And Jesus went throughout all the cities and villages, teaching in their synagogues and proclaiming the gospel of the kingdom and healing every disease and every affliction. When he saw the crowds, he had compassion for them, because they were harassed and helpless, like sheep without a shepherd. Then he said to his disciples, "The harvest is plentiful, but the laborers are few; therefore pray earnestly to the Lord of the harvest to send out laborers into his harvest." (Matt. 9:35–38 ESV)

In Mark 16:15, Jesus commands, "Go into all the world and preach the gospel to all creation." In Luke 19:9–10, he says, "Today salvation has come to this house, because this man, too, is a son of Abraham. For the Son of Man came to seek and to save the lost." I see it in John 4:13–14 when he tells the Samaritan woman that "everyone who drinks this water will be thirsty again, but whoever drinks the water I give them will never thirst. Indeed, the water I give them will become in them a spring of water welling up to eternal life."

It is clear to me that Jesus was committed to reaching everyone with

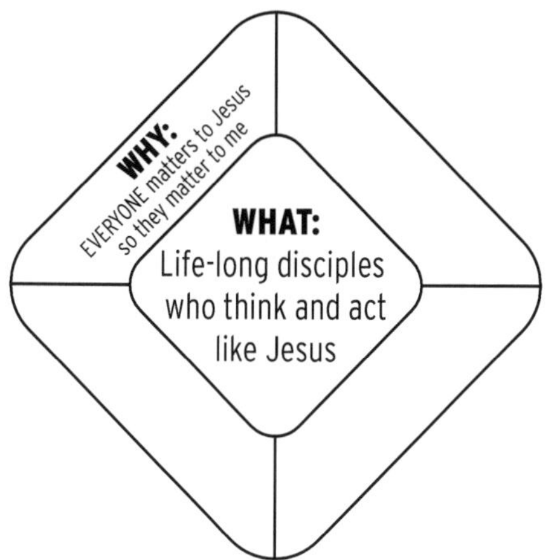

the message of hope and forgiveness, that he cared about people who did not know him or were not a part of his following at that time. And what about John 3:16? Is there any doubt that we are to follow in the footsteps of Jesus and do ministry with everyone?

If everyone matters to Jesus, everyone matters to me.

WORSHIP AND THE WORD?

Looking at the life of Jesus, it becomes clear that he embraced community with his believers. He did this through worship and the opening of the Word. For some of you, this will resonate in a special way. You love your sense of community with people in your church. They provide you with a sense of belonging. You may have that unique gift to lead in worship through music and the spoken word. You may be that person that others love to hear talk or the one who is a great singer. Some of us aren't great speakers or singers, and that's okay!

I grew up in a church that most would consider small. For my siblings and me, it was an amazing ministry. We didn't have a youth pastor, but we had people who loved us and led the ministry for youth very well. It didn't matter what was going on, what the activity was, or even if there was a blizzard outside—we were going to youth group. I was reminiscing with my sister Becky about one particular Sunday night while I was away at college. She begged our mom to drive her to youth group regardless of the extreme winter conditions. Finally, my mom relented. Why? She knew how much that community of believers meant to her daughter. They only made it a few miles before the car slid into a ditch and had to get pulled out. Even after all of that, Becky insisted they carry on to church.

This was our experience. We had a genuine community. It didn't matter the location of this church, how many people attended, or how "cool" the space was. What mattered to us was having a place where we felt loved and like we belonged. Our common denominator was not what schools we attended, the amount of money our parents made, who was cool and who was not, or even the style of clothes we wore. Our common denominator was Jesus.

Who exemplified community more than Jesus? In Matthew 18:20, Jesus says, "For where two or three are gathered in my name, there am I among them" (ESV). In Luke 2 we see Jesus connecting with people as a child.

> Every year Jesus' parents went to Jerusalem for the Festival of the Passover. When he was twelve years old, they went up to the festival, according to the custom. After the festival was over, while his parents were returning home, the boy Jesus stayed behind in Jerusalem, but they were unaware of it. Thinking he was in their company, they traveled on for a day. Then they began looking for him among their relatives and friends. When they did not find him, they went back to Jerusalem to look for him. After three days they found him in the temple courts, sitting among the teachers, listening to them and asking them questions. Everyone who heard him was amazed at his understanding and his answers. (Luke 2:41–47)

Is there anything more sacred for a body of believers than communing together, such as during the Last Supper?

As they were eating, he took bread, and after blessing it broke it and gave it to them, and said, "Take; this is my body." And he took a cup, and when he had given thanks he gave it to them, and they all drank of it. And he said to them, "This is my blood of the covenant, which is poured out for many. Truly, I say to you, I will not drink again of the fruit of the vine until that day when I drink it new in the kingdom of God." (Mark 14:22–25 ESV)

It's clear that Jesus desires those who call him Lord to gather together and worship. Even after his time on earth as a physical presence was over, his desire for us to gather and worship only intensified. We see this in Hebrews:

Therefore, brothers, since we have confidence to enter the holy places by the blood of Jesus, by the new and living way that he opened for us through the curtain, that is, through his flesh, and since we have a great priest over the house of God, let us draw near with a true heart in full assurance of faith, with our hearts sprinkled clean from an evil conscience and our bodies washed with pure water. Let us hold fast the confession of our hope without wavering, for he who promised is faithful. And let us consider how to stir up one another to love and good works, not neglecting to meet together, as is the habit of some, but encouraging one another, and all the more as you see the Day drawing near. (Heb. 10:19–25 ESV)

What about Jesus as a worshiper? We see that worship was foundational for the culture he was raised in. Jesus went to the synagogue with his disciples and was asked to read Scripture. Luke 4:16–19 ESV records this:

And he came to Nazareth, where he had been brought up. And as was his custom, he went to the synagogue on the Sabbath day, and he stood up to read. And the scroll of the prophet Isaiah was given to him. He unrolled the scroll and found the place where it was written,

> "The Spirit of the Lord is upon me,
>> because he has anointed me
>> to proclaim good news to the poor.
> He has sent me to proclaim liberty to the captives
>> and recovering of sight to the blind,
>> to set at liberty those who are oppressed,
> to proclaim the year of the Lord's favor."

The leader of the synagogue could call on anyone to read the Scripture, and here, it was Jesus who was called on. This is just another example of how Jesus was part of the body before he revealed himself to them as something much more. Jesus didn't invent worship, he participated in it. Jesus actively participated with people in worshiping.

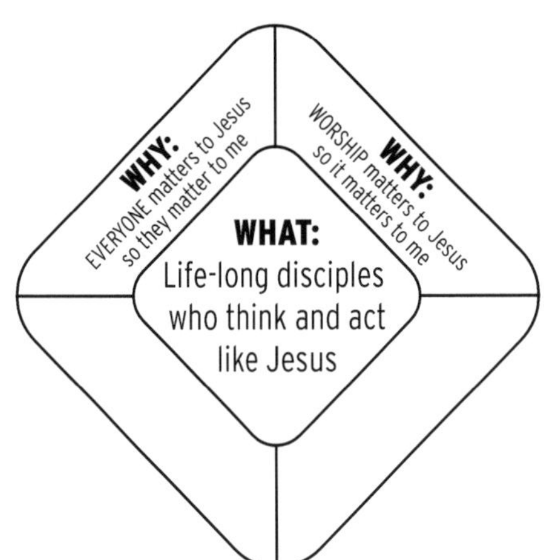

He didn't come on the scene and say "Worship me." He first modeled worship by the way he worshiped his Father.

If worship matters to Jesus, worship matters to me.

SPIRITUAL GROWTH AND CHARACTER CHANGE

The beauty of the gospel is that Jesus not only saves us, but he also makes us new. He doesn't leave us stuck in our sin, doomed to keep repeating destructive patterns of behavior that hurt ourselves and others until he returns or our time on earth is done. As we follow Jesus, learning what he did and what mattered to him and putting it into practice, we are changed from the inside out. The Holy Spirit changes our hearts to look more and more like Jesus' heart. As we learn God's ways through his Word, we find our desires change: we start caring about the things that mattered to Jesus. Our relationships change: we start treating people selflessly, serving them the way Jesus did. Our sense of purpose changes: we start engaging in his kingdom work of making all things new. In short, he changes our character.

This spiritual transformation often happens best in the context of deep, transparent relationships where you can be real about where you are growing and where you are falling short of Jesus' way. It means studying the Word to learn the Father's heart and his ways—just like Jesus did. It means figuring out together what it looks like to choose God's way over our way and then putting it into practice together, keeping one another accountable for our choices and actions. Eventually, as the Holy Spirit changes our hearts, we grow in our faith and God's ways become our ways.

In my ministry, I have always been connected to a wide range of people at different stages of their spiritual development. I have led discipleship groups for middle school students as well as groups for those who have been growing in their faith for upwards of seventy years. I've found that there are important differences in how discipleship looks for people at different stages of faith. With middle school groups, the great challenge was getting at least five minutes of deep conversation. It could take forty-five minutes to work up to the really deep five minutes. Some parents said it seemed like there was more "playtime" in those groups than anything else. I would beg to differ. For a group like that, the point was facilitating the opportunity for deeper conversation, and on good days, that's what happened. Even though they may not have all retained the specific spiritual lessons taught in those instances, what many of them would go on to remember is the sense of community and acceptance fostered there.

The older group I mentioned was very different. We would meet together at six in the morning and couldn't wait to dig deep into God's Word—as long as we had coffee first. The local Starbucks was slammed with groups meeting around tables inside and out. That group would climb to the top of Mount Everest in shorts and T-shirts to show their commitment to the discipleship group. You want to know what's weird? Years later we would gather and, if you didn't have your notes with you, it would be hard to remember all the great biblical truths that were shared. What we all remembered was the commitment we had made to one another to grow in our faith. Sound familiar? The truth for both groups is this: God's Word does not return void. Intentional time spent digging deeper into God's Word rests not on our capacity to retain it all. It rests on the fact that his supernatural truth will reveal itself later down the road in our lives.

Jesus began his ministry by starting with a small group of followers learning to do what he did:

> While walking by the Sea of Galilee, he saw two brothers, Simon (who is called Peter) and Andrew his brother, casting a net into the sea, for they were fishermen. And he said to them, "Follow me, and I will make you fishers of men." Immediately they left their nets and followed him. (Matt. 4:18–20 ESV)

Remember the feeding of the 5,000? These were some of the same disciples who had to grow in their knowledge and faith. We see where it starts here in Matthew, and we see how years later they still needed to grow. Discipleship is a process. Some would also say it's a destination. If both are true, then it's the passage between the beginning and the end. It's through the journey that we learn all of our lessons.

What we also see here in Matthew 4 is Jesus inviting people to come follow him. Jesus didn't tell them where to go; he is not a road sign that just points in one direction. He is leading the way and inviting them to follow. This begs the question: Why would anyone want to follow us? If they follow us, where are they going to end up?

Skip was a guy going somewhere. When I think about it, Skip was a guy who had been everywhere. So why was he driven to keep going? It seemed like he had everything and, at his age, could have shut it down and hung out at the beach all day. But that wasn't Skip. Regardless of the pain in his life and the loss of his wife Sally, Skip kept moving ahead. So many of us followed. There were times when he talked about Jesus while not looking at us listeners. It was as if he was talking directly to Jesus, and we were simply spectators to the conversation. We would talk behind Skip's back, saying that we wanted what he had. Being discipled by Skip was a process of trying to keep up with him spiritually. Skip was mimicking Jesus. He didn't tell us what to do and then sit down. He told us what to do and then he went and did it. He was a person who understood discipleship. We don't need people telling us just what to do; we need people doing it and then inviting us to join them.

Scripture is filled with great examples of discipleship. In Luke 9:23, Jesus says, "Whoever wants to be my disciple must deny themselves and take up their cross daily and follow me." In John 8:31–32, he says, "If you hold to my teaching, you are really my disciples. Then you will know the truth, and the truth will set you free."

For Jesus, discipleship was helping his followers understand who he was. Like so many of us, they felt unworthy of being called a disciple at that time. What had they done to earn the title? Even more, how many times did they fail at doing what Jesus had asked them to do? Don't forget, these people were with Jesus every day in person. It still took them years to truly grow in their understanding of Jesus and learn what it meant to be a follower of Jesus. Embracing the process of spiritual growth and character change is the action of a person who understands that they are a child of God and that he is the source of power and strength. For most of my life I went to an altar (or just a quiet place) asking Jesus to save me—to forgive me—without getting up and walking away with his grace, empowered to change. The list of things that we are to learn, that we are to become, is not something that any one of us can accomplish on our own. We need his grace and mercy in our lives as we submit to his truth and power as well.

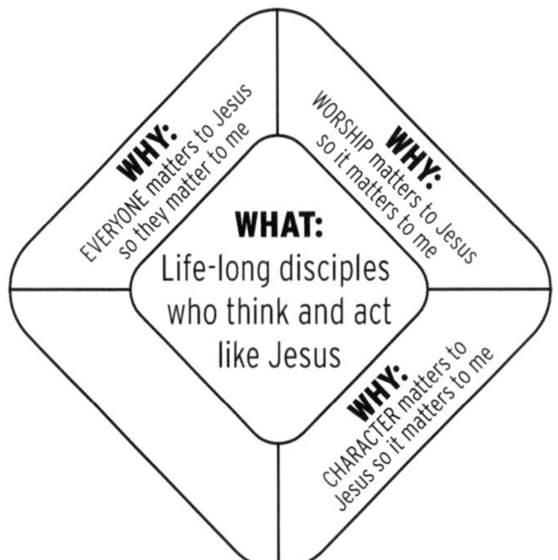

If character mattered to Jesus, character matters to me.

WHO IS A LEADER?

Let's go back to the feeding of the 5,000, specifically to when Jesus asks the disciples to take the baskets and distribute the food among the people. Remember the context of this event. There are twelve baskets and some 18,000 people. You can imagine the level of anxiety that is racing through the veins of each disciple as they are faced with distributing so little food to so many people. The big lesson here is that they put their faith in Jesus into action. This is the next step in the development of the disciples.

I've heard many times, like you might have, that we must not only be hearers of the Word but doers as well. We talk about faith and works going hand in hand, but what does it take for a person to become a leader?

Is it a strong voice? A strong opinion? Is it something passed down from a family member? What do we see in Scripture? What is the secret?

> Jesus called them to him and said, "You know that the rulers of the Gentiles lord it over them, and their great ones exercise authority over them. It shall not be so among you. But whoever would be great among you must be your servant, and whoever would be first among you must be your slave, even as the Son of Man came not to be served but to serve, and to give his life as a ransom for many." (Matt. 20:25–28 ESV)

Biblical leadership is something that is revealed in a person as much as it is revered. Biblical leadership grows out of a desire to use what you have been given and then share that gift with others. We see clearly in Matthew that a leader must first be a servant, one willing to consider the needs of others ahead of his or her own. This is a very radical concept because it stands against the popular ideologies of power and control. Biblical leadership can be so confusing as it does not fit into a stereotype, and it is not limited to a certain number of people. Biblical leadership occurs when a person who is being discipled comes to understand their gifts and talents, then maximizes them for the glory of the One who is their author.

During my freshman year of college, I discovered how incredible and smart my mom was. It was Thanksgiving break and I was home for the weekend just a few short weeks before final exams. I was working on a paper and asked her to edit it for me. Before that weekend, I never realized what an accomplished student she had been in high school and college. You see, my mom was a meek person. She waited to speak last and celebrated everyone else before mentioning anything about herself.

She was the top of her class in high school and the school of nursing in college. The only reason she wasn't valedictorian in college is because she didn't want to give a speech, and so she received an A- in one of her classes on purpose.

After that long weekend, I began to see my mom differently and understand some of the things that we are talking about now. I realized that being meek is not the same thing as being weak. In fact, it is the opposite. Her incredible strength lay in that she knew who she was, and she functioned in her strengths. After that discovery, I began to admire how she handled every curveball life threw her way. I began to see that there was more to this person who was my mom. Yes, she was loving and kind in everything she did and with everyone she knew. But she was also the strong woman who carried our family on her back, and only those who lived in that house could see it. She had grace and confidence. When we gathered to say our final goodbyes at her funeral, people filled the church to honor a woman who had impacted their lives as well. That's biblical leadership!

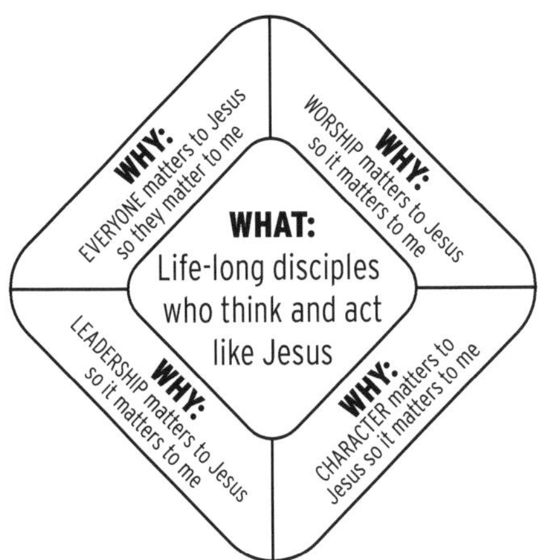

We have all been given gifts and talents. The question is, how do we use them? Jesus clearly speaks to this in the parable of the talents. In Matthew 25, Jesus puts the emphasis on what we do with what we have been given, not how much we have been given. This is where we help people in our ministry understand that the preconceived idea of a leader is not the same as what is presented in Scripture. I used to think that I needed the most outspoken person to lead all areas of ministry, but failed to understand that leadership is as much about stewardship as it is personality.

If leadership matters to Jesus, leadership matters to me.

LET'S REVIEW

If we can agree on the answer to three core questions of biblical strategy, we can be more unified as the church. I think we all agree on *what* we are called to do: Jesus clearly called us to make disciples. Our mission is to help people become lifelong followers of Jesus who think and act like him. Everything we do ties back to this goal. But from this point we get offtrack and follow our own ways to achieve the goal. Instead of focusing on *why* and *how* Jesus made disciples, we get caught up in the latest ministry trends, chasing after things we see succeed in other ministry contexts. We might even focus on one aspect of how Jesus ministered, but we end up with an unbalanced ministry that fails to make the big impact in students' lives that it could if we would only look at how Jesus modeled a balanced ministry.

I believe a biblical strategy answers three core questions: *What, Why,* and *How?* The answers to these questions are the same for all of us and they were modeled by Jesus. *What* are we called to do? Make disciples. *Why* is it important? Jesus showed us by his example that everyone matters to him, so everyone matters to us. Worship matters to him, so it matters to us. Character—spiritual growth and heart transformation—matters to Jesus, so it matters to us. Leadership—using spiritual gifts in service to others—matters to Jesus, so it matters to us. These core beliefs motivate us in our calling to make disciples. The answer to the *Why* question is: it matters to Jesus, so it matters to us.

Then we look at the ways Jesus ministered to find the answer to *how*. He gathered in community for worship and teaching. He walked together with a few to practice God's ways and to help them experience heart transformation and grow in their character. He empowered people for ministry, giving them opportunities to serve others. He reached out to meet people where they were. Jesus modeled all these methods, often simultaneously. For example, he empowered his close followers, the twelve disciples, for ministry while teaching the crowds, as we discussed in the story of feeding the 5,000.

These answers to *What*, *Why*, and *How* provide a biblical strategy for ministry that unifies us all. When we move to the next group of questions, *Who*, *When*, and *Where*, we differ in the details. These are tactics, and tactics are changeable based on our contexts, resources, and abilities. And therein lies the beauty of ministry. We can be unified in a biblical strategy and diverse in our tactics for our unique ministry context as we answer the *Who*, *When*, and *Where* questions.

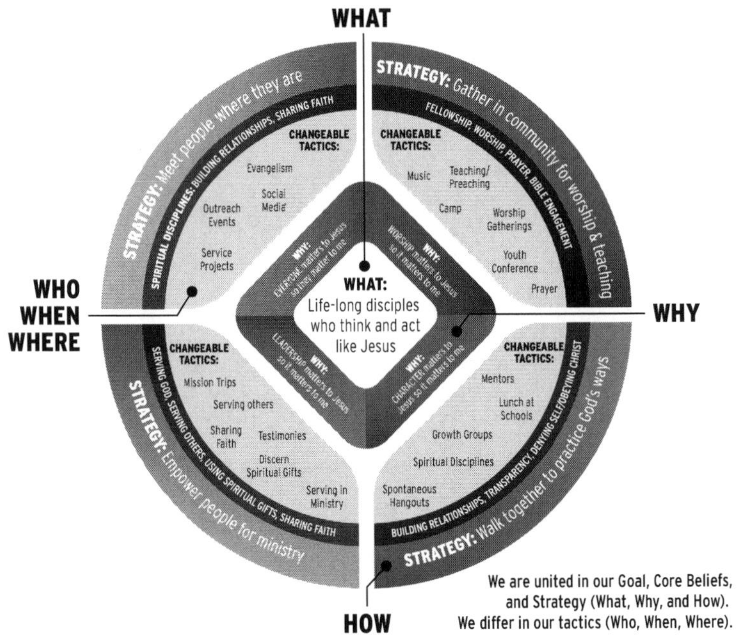

THINK TACTICAL

FULL CIRCLE

THINK TACTICAL

AT A SMALL LEADERSHIP CONFERENCE in Orlando, Florida, a group of ministry leaders and I gathered to learn from each other and listen to speakers who offered different perspectives from our own. One of those speakers, Michael Lingerfelt, left a lasting impression on me. I came to believe that he was one of the most creative and gifted people in the world in my estimation.

When Michael was in the early years of his craft as an architect, he became what is known as a "Disney Imagineer." Walt Disney (you know, the creator of Mickey Mouse) developed the Imagineers as a group of people who could help him build his amazing Disney brand. One of their creations was Disney's Animal Kingdom Theme Park at Walt Disney World Resort in Bay Lake, Florida, the largest park of its kind in the world. Michael began telling us the story of how the design of Animal Kingdom became a reality and the challenges that came along with building something of such scale, specifically the centerpiece of the park—the Tree of Life. At 145-feet tall, the massive baobab sculpture was developed as the main theme and crossroads where all walking paths led. He shared so many great stories about the project that I could hardly keep up, but two points he made that day are burned into my memory.

First, he said that when building anything, from a major theme park to a church ministry, we should "always begin with the end in mind." He talked about *why* he wanted to design Animal Kingdom and *why* that massive tree was so important. Sound familiar from the first part of this book? He needed everything designed in that park to point to the tree. He wanted every color and every street sign in the park to reflect what it was all built around. He said that once you know the *why*, then you can begin to construct the what, when, where, and how that will help you get there.

The second thing Michael said that stuck with me is "help people see the future." He explained to us that people are so overwhelmed with the circumstances of life that they can't see what's right in front of them. It's our job to show them that there's so much more if they just look up. They need someone like us to come along and clear the path. He told us to build something and pave the way for them to get there, just like the tagline from the movie *Field of Dreams*: If you build it, they will come. What Michael did for those of us gathered that day was help establish our purpose in the strategy (the *What*, *Why*, and *How*) so we could be creative and wise with the tactics (the *Who*, *Where*, and *When*). Make no mistake, the strategy was the heart of all that he built and the *Who*, *Where*, and *When* were simply the vehicle to help people get there.

The rest of this section is dedicated to exactly that—the *Who*, *When*, and *Where*. The answers to these questions are what we call *tactics*. They are the building blocks of your ministry and the programming that makes it possible for people to join in ministry with you. But I will warn you, programming is misunderstood in some circles because people confuse programming with mission or core values. Programming has been mistaken as the heart of ministry, and for some, even the reason we do ministry. Programming is not the *Why*, it's just a tactic—a way to carry out our biblical strategy. Biblical strategy is our big-picture purpose. Tactics are the detailed, concrete, specific ways we move the strategy forward in our particular ministry context. Once the biblical strategy has been established, programming will help people see the future and how they can get there. I can't state this strongly enough. We must keep tactics in perspective. If they take priority over biblical strategy, then you will have built something doomed to fail. If tactics are in the right place, they help people achieve the vision God has given them and help you to walk with them on that path.

TACTICS GONE WRONG: THE WINTER RETREAT

The winter retreat I had planned was going to be the best one yet. The buses were all lined up, the hotel booked, lift tickets at the ski lodge reserved, and the ministry sessions were going to be incredible. I was sure God was going to move in big ways that weekend. But it all started to unravel once the buses pulled out of town. I wasn't prepared for some of the language on the bus, and it didn't get any better from there. Once we got to the hotel, it was a struggle to keep some students from trashing their rooms. When we all gathered in the conference room for the first session (one I was sure would be epic), some students talked during worship and our guest speaker struggled to rise above the noise. Afterwards, we got everyone in their rooms and hoped the next day would be better. The plan was to hit the slopes and keep the students busy, hoping that would solve some of our problems. To make matters worse, several of my student leaders talked to me that night and expressed concern over some of the behavior being exhibited. They wanted the worship to dig deeper, but the distractions made that difficult for even the most spiritually mature among them. I promised them it would get better the next day, but it didn't. The evening session at the ski resort was only better because some of the students were so tired that they slept during the worship and message. We made it through the night with no issues. I can't describe the relief of loading up the buses the next morning. We made the long drive home without any major conflicts between the staff and students who were determined to use inappropriate language. When we got home and everyone was picked up, I went to my office and cried. How did I fail so miserably in planning this event? This trip was supposed to be the spiritual spark that would take our youth ministry to the next level. The majority of the students on this trip had a great time. They were away from home for the weekend, there was great snow on the slopes, and they liked our guest speaker. But my dream for this event had been for them to have an amazing spiritual experience. I imagined the evening sessions being marked by extended worship and students praying over each other for hours. I imagined a repeat of what we had at a youth camp just six months prior where students were more receptive, sensitive during worship, and making life-changing commitments to follow Jesus. During a staff meeting later that week, I was asked to report how the retreat went and how many students attended. The number was record setting and on paper it was a huge success. But to me it was a failure.

So, what was the real problem? There were several adult leaders at the retreat who wanted to blame a certain group of students for being disruptive and having no respect for me as a pastor. If those students weren't on the trip, they said, it would have been so much better. For a minute I was okay with that until I began to take a deeper look at who those students were. Why wouldn't they follow the rules that were so clearly communicated? The more I looked the more I realized that their actions were their norm. They would go on a spring break trip and nothing I've described was challenged as wrong. Not a problem in their locker rooms. Not a problem in the lunchroom. Not a problem at the school dance. Not a problem at home. Not a problem at parties. I was expecting these students to adjust their behavior because they were on a trip with our ministry, but that simply wasn't reason enough. They weren't problem students or disrespectful teens who wanted to be a disruptive force. They simply didn't share the same values as our other students. Make no mistake, there were plenty of behavioral issues with students who had been part of our ministry for years, but there were different expectations for them and a different level of accountability.

The real problem on that trip was my poor leadership. I didn't understand the makeup of all the students who came along. I was asking students who had never claimed a personal relationship with Jesus to embrace the worship and the Word as if they were seasoned believers. I designed an event that asked students who had never been away from home to conduct themselves as if they were mature adults. I designed an event that wasn't staffed properly and didn't consider all the possible ways that things could go wrong. This event was the last one where I took all those things for granted. I can't say that every event after that was seamless or without issue. What I can say, however, is that it taught me how tactics needed to be implemented to match the biblical strategy of the event.

WHAT MAKES A TACTIC?

Always Changing

Tactics are subject to change. A tactic isn't meant to stand the test of time—that's only for a biblical strategy. Tactics are crafted to be relevant to your specific ministry context and to be reimagined. People used to talk about things called sacred cows—tactics considered to be untouchable for the rest of time. They would say things like, "We always do it this way" or, "That's not the way the leader before you did it." These point to a tactic that has become idolized for fear that God won't move if things change. Don't get me wrong, there are some tactics that have worked really well over time and have been a positive experience for everyone involved. Sometimes tactics are traditions that work year after year. If something is working, that's a good thing; nonetheless, tactics are by their very nature subject to change.

The Thief of Joy

It's been said that comparison is the thief of joy. When you start comparing your ministry with the ones around you, you are in danger of losing what makes you relevant to the people and community that God has given you to shepherd. There is more than one right way to do things. Tactics need to be crafted to serve every area of your ministry strategy; the tactics that work for you might not work for another.

The Copycat

Don't ever think that if you copy what another ministry is doing tactically it will fix the problems you may be having in your own ministry. Remember what unites us is our biblical strategy, not tactics. In fact, tactics might be the area where ministry leaders have failed the most. We hear a great success story from a speaker or read about one in an article and we want that kind of success for ourselves. There's nothing wrong with being inspired by what others are doing; it's important to celebrate how God is using certain leaders and their ministries. What we can't do is simply copy their tactics as if they would fit our specific ministry context. Principles can be transferred, learned, and implemented; however, tactics need to be considered as examples that may or may not function well if mimicked in our own ministry.

Collaboration

Collaboration is working with those within your ministry and those ministries around you; it's not merely copying something and hoping it works. Collaboration is a culture of observing and learning from others—their failures as well as their successes. It's sharing resources and growing in your knowledge of how tactics can be used effectively when implemented correctly. When you desire collaboration with someone and their ministry, you're acknowledging their value in this kingdom work and honoring how God has gifted them to carry it out. One of the greatest gifts we have in ministry is the opportunity to collaborate with others. When this is done in the right spirit, both parties can help move the body of Christ closer to being unified in the all-important task of proclaiming the message of Jesus.

Execution

I'm a football fan and love watching the sport no matter what level it's played at. I go to local high school football games, college football games, professional football games, and even coached my sons' flag football teams. When I walk out on the field of a local high school on a Friday night, the field is 100 yards with two end zones at 10 yards each. That's 120 yards long. The high school field is 53⅓ yards wide from sideline to sideline. On a Saturday, I can walk into a college stadium that seats 107,601 fans, a city in and of itself. The field they play on is 100 yards with two end zones at 10 yards each. That's 120 yards long. The field is 53⅓ yards wide from sideline to sideline. On a Sunday, I can walk into a professional football stadium where they are playing the Super Bowl. The greatest football players in the world are warming up on the field with 100 million people watching. The field they play on is 100 yards with two end zones at 10 yards each. That's 120 yards long. The field is 53⅓ yards wide from sideline to sideline. So, what's the difference? The rules are basically the same, the ball is basically the same, and so are the helmets and pads. What separates high school football, college football, and professional football is execution. The coaches and players have different skill levels, experience, and resources, which impact the tactics they use to play the game, but they all focus on the details and strive for excellence in their contexts. In the same way, ministry leaders are gifted and resourced in different ways, which influences the tactics they design. As you craft tactics that will help students become active in your ministry, you must consider how those tactics can be executed to accomplish your desired outcome.

New Versus Old

Just because something is new to you doesn't mean it's new. Just because something is old doesn't mean it's bad. The goal is to be effective. I was recently at a youth camp where they were playing the same game that I played as a camper in high school. It was the same old game of capture the flag but with a little twist. The camp was located in an incredible wooded area and every year the game was a home run. So why change this tactic and add a twist? Change for the sake of change isn't innovative; it's shortsighted. Take note of the tactics that are working well and have natural momentum. If you have to spend extra energy to get a tactic going, you should consider a change.

Preference Versus Platform

There's no denying that we all have preferences. It really doesn't matter what the topic is; we all have a favorite, traditional, or sentimental viewpoint. There's nothing wrong with having our own preferences, but the problems start when a preference becomes more than it's intended to be and turns into a platform we stand on. When we are in the middle of a debate about who the greatest quarterback of all time is, preference will rule the day. You can make any statistic prove your point or claim that there was a bad call that changed the course of a game. What we can't do is allow a preference to carry the same weight as a biblical principle on which we base our ministry. Our platform has been clearly laid out in Scripture and it unifies us, regardless of the ministry we are part of. Keep preferences where they belong. They are tactics; nothing more and nothing less.

Simplify in Order to Master

Tactics can also help you develop and train students at every level of your ministry and at every level of their development. The beauty of tactics is that you can take one that is very complicated and involved, and simplify it so that students can gain an understanding that will enable them to grow in confidence. Early on in college I was struggling with a piano piece, desperately failing at it regardless of how much time I spent in the practice room. I wasn't a piano major, and I only took basic lessons to fulfill a requirement. One night a music professor heard me playing and popped his head into the practice room. He began to watch me practice, then after a few minutes stopped me. He told me to stop practicing this piece for now, and instead work on my scales and finger work. He started me in the key of C, the most basic key on the piano keyboard. He came back a week later with the sheet music I was learning, but, unlike the original, what he brought was in the key of C. By simplifying the process, he helped me gain some confidence. My playing started to improve, and eventually I succeeded in learning the song. As leaders we must play the same role that professor did and simplify some of our tactics to help our students learn and grow.

One of my favorite quotes is from Albert Einstein: "If you can't explain it simply, you don't understand it well enough." Often the opposite of this is done in ministry. Our tendency is to take a very basic concept and overcomplicate it so that only a few understand. That's a poor tactic. The more that those in our ministry understand, the more they become active. The more they become active, the more they grow as disciples. That's what we want, is it not? Simplify some things so that the students we shepherd can learn and grow.

One Size Doesn't Fit All

Every community carries its own unique culture with it, and that culture must be understood if we want to create tactics that actually work. This applies to the students and to the leaders who are part of your ministry. Understanding their personalities and backgrounds will go a long way towards helping you identify tactics that complement them. When you take both personality and background into consideration, you can implement multiple tactics at the same time.

During the first half of my ministry, I just assumed that the correct tactic for reaching everyone was a big event. The more people in the room, the bigger the response to the invitation of salvation, I thought. I've witnessed this happen in some very large gatherings, and I have seen God move through those crowds firsthand. There's nothing wrong with this tactic; however, there is more than one right way to implement it. In my first ministry, we didn't have a big group or a dedicated youth ministry space. We didn't have the budget that would allow us to bring in a great band or speaker. On the other hand, we did have a community with many schools and other opportunities for outreach. There was a Dairy Queen near the church, a big open space behind the church, and a neighborhood across the street. I had to learn how to appreciate the resources around me and figure out how they could be used as tools to help me in the broader biblical strategy of reaching more students.

I remember going to a high school basketball game to see one of the students in the youth group play, and I was surrounded by a few thousand other students. It took attending a few games for me to realize that being together in one space was a legitimate tactic. I began using what little budget I had to buy popcorn and pass it out. It was something to break the ice and start a conversation. I would ask students from our ministry to sit with me and do the same, starting with their friends. It was a tactic. At another ministry years later, we would pass out coffee and donuts in a school parking lot. A tactic. I booked a big band and a great speaker. A tactic. I gave away cars once a year to encourage our students to bring their friends. A tactic. I would take students home in the church van, stopping at the store to buy beverages so that I could see their neighborhoods and understand their lives a little better. A tactic. For those ministries, these were the right tactics based on what was relevant and beneficial at the time, and they served a single purpose based on a specific biblical strategy.

Open the Next Door

When designing and organizing events in ministry, we must consider what is next. Where do we want these students to go? Depending on what biblical strategy you are creating tactics for, you must always keep the end in mind. One of the greatest examples of this is how we design youth camps. If you are like me, you grew up going to a camp that you absolutely loved. Great memories, right? I've had many conversations with pastors and students about what nights were their favorite at youth camp. What was their favorite song or tradition? Almost all of us remember the last night at camp when we all got saved. This happened to me every year of camp, and yes, I went down front and it was a Friday night. That last night, people cried and hugged. We promised each other that we would never go back to doing things the way we did before camp. This year was going to be different. Then we all asked Jesus into our hearts again. The truth is, I was already saved, I just wasn't growing in my faith.

As a youth pastor, I struggled with this when designing my own camps and speaking at other camps. The big change came when we took a deep look at who was going to camp and where they were in their spiritual journey. We compared that information to what the design of the camp was and saw the problem. Most of the students attending had already accepted Jesus, and yet the majority of our camp was designed to provide an opportunity for that to happen. After all, getting saved is all that camps are good for, right? The first big step was to organize our students into cabins with a leader that would continue discipling once camp was over. A tactic. Why not take advantage of all that camp time, the most dedicated time that we have with students all year? Did we have an evening service with an invitation to know Jesus for the first time? Absolutely. However, we did this on the second night—not the last one. We made it clear that there was a standing invitation to accept Jesus, regardless of the day or time. This one small change began to have a significant impact after camp was over. For the students, camp was the end of the summer and the last big event. It was the pinnacle of our programming and the momentum carried everyone forward, especially the graduates. For them, it may have been their last youth group experience before entering a new stage of spiritual growth. For the ministry in general, camp was a launching point and set the stage for what the next year was going to be like. This can be true for any event you design, regardless of where it's placed in your ministry.

Where does a mission trip fit into all this, and who should go on that trip? Is it an open invitation, or do you design it for students based on where they are in their spiritual journey? Why not have two mission trips? One with students who are in discipleship groups and designed to help them become leaders in this ministry, and another with students who are already in leadership positions that you want to really dig deep with. It's simply the tactics that make this work. The first trip can be close to home, the other one out of the country.

Retreats are great events to design for what's next. Why not take a day trip with students who are new to your ministry? Another trip can be designed to do the same thing I just talked about with missions' trips, but on a much larger scale and more affordable. Depending on the school calendar, a perfectly placed retreat can really help reenergize your students.

See where I'm going with all of this? Everything you design in your ministry should help students walk through the next door of your ministry model. Every other area of their life is designed to change with them as they mature and grow. We see this in the school system, the sports leagues, the performing arts, and all the other extracurriculars. Our responsibility as a leader is to design a ministry that encourages students to grow and gives them opportunities along the way.

GOD'S WORD DOESN'T RETURN VOID

So shall my word be that goes out from my mouth; it shall not return to me empty, but it shall accomplish that which I purpose, and shall succeed in the thing for which I sent it.
—Isaiah 55:11 ESV

What happens if your students don't walk through the next door? What happens if they don't want to move at all? This may be one of the greatest challenges in youth ministry. You can't force them in their spiritual journey, you can only encourage them. Here's when we must rely on the promise made in Isaiah 55. As difficult as it is, we must stay committed to the ministry we have been given. We must honor Christ by our commitment to his Word. He is the one that draws all people to himself, and we are simply tools in that process.

I remember a meeting with the other pastors on a student ministries team. We had just had a great retreat, and the entire year was planned out. We had it all organized. We were convinced that the next year was going to be the best ever. Students could come to know Jesus and get connected every weekend service. They could engage with a great discipleship group, read through the Bible in a year, discover their gifts and talents in our leadership training events, and become a model leader. All this could be accomplished if they just committed to our ministry plan, we thought. Yet we failed to consider that none of us on the pastoral team had accomplished that in one year (or two years, or three) when we were students. The reality is that every student is unique; they move and progress in their relationship with Jesus at their own pace. We must craft a ministry that is built for natural growth and development in the lives of students, and we must be ready when students are ready for that next step.

TACTICS DEFINED

I started this section saying that tactics answer the *Who*, *When*, and *Where* questions—who we are trying to reach, when we do ministry, and where we do ministry. Tactics are the programming details of how we accomplish the strategy. Tactics are subject to change, and they should be designed to fit your unique ministry context. Remember, the *What*, *Why*, and *How* questions are not tactics, they are the biblical strategy. I want to dig a little deeper now and define tactics that align with the ministry strategy outlined in the first section on Biblical Strategy.

TACTICS AND EVERYONE:
Evangelism and Outreach with Salvation

> *Jesus said to him, "Today salvation has come to this house,*
> *because this man, too, is a son of Abraham. For the Son of*
> *Man came to seek and to save the lost."*
> *—Luke 19:9–10*

We've established that everyone refers to all people inside and outside of our ministry. The common denominator is that everyone is born with a sinful nature and needs the life-giving power of Jesus. Two of the broader tactics used by the church to help people know Jesus are evangelism and outreach. With this in mind, we want to design these tactics with the goal of introducing students to Jesus. These tactics have one basic thing in common: a need for an established relationship. This relationship might begin with you, a student in your ministry, or another leader, but the goal is ultimately that the student is introduced to Jesus. Then, when a student makes a commitment to Jesus, they have opened the door to the rest of their life with Jesus as the center. We often say they do it with "all their heart, mind, and soul." That's salvation, and it's the first step toward spiritual maturity. The name Jesus (derived from the Hebrew Yeshua, meaning "to deliver" or "to rescue") itself means salvation.

TACTICS AND WORSHIP:
Gathering and Community with Accountability

> *But the hour is coming, and is now here, when the true worshipers will worship the Father in spirit and truth, for the Father is seeking such people to worship him. God is spirit, and those who worship him must worship in spirit and truth.*
> *—John 4:23–24 ESV*

As a noun, worship is the inward disposition toward God as the highest love of our hearts. It's the total offering of ourselves to him because he alone is worthy. As a verb, worship consists of teaching and studying the Word, praying, participating in the eucharistic meal, and fellowshipping with other believers. Music and song are vehicles, among many others, to offer praise and worship to the Lord. Worship can't be confined to any Sunday service alone. It must reach into our everyday lives through daily personal adoration and in loving our neighbor.

In a youth ministry context, worship is the way in which a student, who accepts Jesus as Lord and Savior, walks in fellowship with other believers. The tactics used to facilitate this worship are gathering and community, and they describe what happens when the body of Christ comes together. A student needs consistency and accountability, which are natural expressions of a healthy, biblical worship experience. Spiritual disciplines that need to be active in the student's life to help them move to the next level of spiritual maturity are prayer, worship, fellowship, and participating in community.

TACTICS AND DISCIPLESHIP:
Spiritual Development with Transformation

> *Therefore go and make disciples of all nations, baptizing*
> *them in the name of the Father and of the Son and of the*
> *Holy Spirit, and* teaching them to obey everything I have
> commanded you. *And surely I am with you always,*
> *to the very end of the age.*
> *—Matthew 28:19–20*

We are to spread this good news everywhere—to the ends of the earth—secure that Jesus is with us always. As students discover Jesus and choose to follow him (that's the definition of a disciple), the Great Commission tells us our job is to teach them to obey what he taught. As they do what he did and taught, they learn to think and act like Jesus. The Holy Spirit does his work to transform their hearts to look more and more like Jesus. "The student is not above the teacher, but everyone who is fully trained will be like their teacher" (Luke 6:40).

Discipleship as a ministry means we are teaching students God's way—what following Jesus looks like. Tactically, this may mean one-on-one mentoring relationships, small groups, or the messages we share in larger group settings. It might include serving others together, side-by-side, doing what Jesus did. It might mean giving them opportunities to practice sharing about their faith journey and pointing others to the discovery of Jesus.

The expectations for students at this stage of their spiritual development needs to be understood in the context of an adolescent and not a fully mature person. The process of developing and maturing as a human carries its own complicated developmental concerns. How do we help a student who loves and desires to serve Jesus grow spiritually in the midst of the most aggressive physical, mental, and social changes of their life? This understanding in no way waters down the expectations we have for students. It simply helps us better realize what those expectations should be during this stage, and guides how we walk with students if they don't meet them.

The tactics used here help students understand God's design for their life and practice doing what Jesus did. Spiritual disciplines that need to be active in the student's life to help them move to the next level of spiritual maturity involve engaging with what Jesus taught and putting it into practice: studying the Word, denying self, and choosing God's way over our way (obedience). Students also need deep relationships where they can experience transparency and accountability.

TACTICS AND LEADERSHIP:
Gifts and Talents with Purpose

But you are not to be like that. Instead, the greatest among you should be like the youngest, and the one who rules like the one who serves. For who is greater, the one who is at the

table or the one who serves? Is it not the one who is at the
table? But I am among you as one who serves.
—*Luke 22:26–27*

The definition of leadership in this book is a student who, in the process of growing in their faith and understanding of Jesus, is discovering how they can use their gifts and talents to serve God and others. We often hear the term *servant leadership* to describe this process. The main distinction of leadership as a follower of Christ is grounded in the posture of leadership as a servant. This posture is what makes Christian leadership unique. The entire process of leadership operates under the lordship of Christ. This process is not about position or power; it's about discovering gifts and talents and allowing them to be used for God's purposes.

The tactics that facilitate leadership involve serving others with *gifts* and *talents*. Every student has them, and learning to use and understand them will be tools that they will use to lead and serve others in ministry. The spiritual disciplines that need to be active in students' lives to help them move to the next level of spiritual maturity involve *purpose*: serving God, serving others, using spiritual gifts, and sharing their faith.

THINK
PRACTICAL

FULL CIRCLE

THINK PRACTICAL

BOB BUILDS GUITARS. HIS ENTIRE adult life has been this wild journey of crafting an instrument that has been around for centuries in one form or another. I played a guitar before I ever met Bob. I remember opening a box Christmas morning to find the most beautiful thing I had ever laid my eyes on. I still remember the smell. The guitar came with a book of chord charts and songs. I spent Christmas day mastering "Country Roads" by John Denver, playing until my fingers were raw. I had experience with guitars and owned a few, but when I met Bob everything I understood about guitars changed when I saw the wood before it became the instrument. I saw behind the curtain and my eyes were opened to what it meant to be a craftsman.

On one of my visits to talk to Bob, he cut the meeting short and took me for a walk around the shop. We went into a room that was small and out of the way. In that room was a bunch of pieces, but no fully formed guitars. Pointing to different pieces, Bob explained how they each played a specific role in the design of the guitar. Bob was also constantly designing new guitars and making improvements. However, the improvements didn't always go as planned as some new parts were flawed in some form or fashion. Strikingly, Bob would never consider these pieces as failures. In fact, he showed me another room full of these flawed pieces and as we walked around, he recounted to me the lessons they represented. And then Bob pointed to a particular piece on the wall and told me about how it would work with another particular piece and become something amazing and worth playing. Bob wasn't thwarted by the failures; he was driven by learning lessons that would bring him closer to success, as little as that might be in that moment. I walked around with him, soaking in his experience and wisdom and began to understand that he was helping me understand ministry as much as he was teaching me about making a guitar. I learned that ministry is this dance of success and failure. Neither one can define you as both will always be close by your side. The key is learning the lessons that success and failure can teach you so that you can apply what you learn days, months, or even years down the road.

What lessons have you learned already? What successes or failures have made you wiser in your understanding of how to improve as a leader—ones that will help students navigate their way around some of the most imposing obstacles that lie ahead of them?

In this section, I want to walk you through a room like Bob's, but instead of guitar pieces, it's lined with ministry experiences, ones that I have learned from and ones that I hope will help you as you build your own ministry. There is always room on my walls as I learn and grow in real time, and that's what I want for you as well.

The common thread is "fitting all the pieces together" to create a framework for ministry. I have asked youth ministry veterans and a few students who are walking beside me, to join in this investment in you. I believe that information can be gleaned, it can be googled, you can read it, and even take a test on it. However, the gateway to understanding ministry (and really anything) is only through the door of living and suffering through it. There is no other way to say it: You must spend time—years of it—in ministry to really have some level of understanding. The people who have joined me in this section have lived and suffered in ministry. Learn from them.

THINK CULTURE

by Stacy Shaw

CULTURE HAPPENS

Every youth ministry has a culture. The culture may be warm and inviting, or it may be cliquish or standoffish. But like anything we are entrenched in, it can be challenging to know the culture of the youth ministry until we step back, make observations, and ask hard questions. Understanding culture and taking steps to shape culture are essential tasks of the youth worker.

A key word when we think about culture is intentionality. Culture is going to happen, so we need to intentionally influence the type of culture teens experience when they engage in the youth ministry. Youth pastors, youth leaders, and key teens play an important role in creating culture. Why does culture matter so much? The culture of the ministry can impact the effectiveness of the ministry's evangelism and discipleship efforts. A youth worker may put months into planning a retreat for their high school students in hopes of attracting new students who might come to know Jesus as their Savior. However, the preparation won't matter if a new student feels like an outsider and decides to leave because they are having a crummy time.

THE GOLD STANDARD

While youth workers should want their youth ministries to be attractive to outsiders, it isn't enough to just pursue a culture of niceness. Youth workers should seek to root the culture of their ministries in Jesus and the early church. When we look at how Jesus interacted with people and how the early church functioned, we see the type of biblical culture we should strive to cultivate in our ministries.

A CULTURE OF BELONGING

The Christian life is not meant to be lived alone. Humans were created for community with God and with others. This means the Christian faith is both individual and communal. Community matters because we are better together. Life with others helps believers to stay accountable to life with God. Proverbs 27:17 tells us, "As iron sharpens iron, so one person sharpens another." Additionally, community matters because God often communicates with us through other believers around us. Community is essential to the Christian faith.

Everyone longs to belong somewhere. Teenagers especially are looking for a place they can belong and be loved. Youth ministries need to cultivate a culture of inclusion. It needs to be a place where any teenager can say, "These are my people. I am loved here."

Throughout the New Testament, Jesus communicates that he does not discriminate. He welcomes the poor, the oppressed, the elite, and the marginalized to be in relationship with him. During Jesus' day, most rabbis only allowed men to be their students. However, Jesus also welcomed women to be his disciples. We clearly see this when he spends time at Martha's house and affirms Mary sitting at his feet, taking the posture of a disciple (Luke 10:38–42). A biblical culture welcomes all types of people into community.

Youth workers must look honestly at their youth ministries and determine if any groups of teens may feel left out, whether based on age, school, gender, race, sexual orientation, family dynamics, or physical or mental disability. Youth workers might find it helpful to interview core and uninvolved students to find out what helps and hinders belonging. We all have blind spots. It could be that the youth ministry program is created for extroverts, not introverts, or programming elements are not designed for teens with ability limitations.

Once you identify a blind spot, do everything you can to address it. Part of this is preaching and creating avenues for discussions on belonging and embracing others. Consider challenging your teens to actively embrace people different than them. Model for them and teach them how to converse with people where they find common ground. Challenge them to get to know one another more personally and create spaces for relationships to be built. Think about how you might handle rooming assignments, van rides, volunteer roles, and small groups to help teens get to know each other better.

In John 19:25–27, Scripture tells us that while in the agony of crucifixion, Jesus found it important enough to use his precious breath to bring his mother, Mary, and his disciple, John, into community. Jesus connected them to one another for the purpose of belonging and community. One way that youth workers can help create a culture of belonging is to constantly look for ways to connect people to people. Consistently work to connect teens with other teens or with adults who they can relate to and invest in a friendship with. When a student tells you they are really into cars, and you personally know nothing about cars, intentionally connect them to another leader who relates with their passions. Connecting people to people creates a culture where everyone knows they can belong and be loved.

A CULTURE OF HONOR

Jesus honored young people. He invited young disciples to follow him and assigned the early church to their care. Jesus' mother herself was a teenager when she was entrusted to be pregnant with the Son of God. Jesus honored young people and saw them as full participants in the kingdom of God.

Does your youth ministry honor teens in their specific stage of life? Often, adults in the church see young people as problems that need to be fixed. They focus on ministry to teenagers instead of viewing youth ministry as ministry with teenagers. A biblical culture will look at young people and see them as full participants in the kingdom of God now. Youth workers should strive to create spaces for teens to develop their gifts and talents. This means things might happen differently than if you did them yourself. Different is not bad! Honoring teens means challenging them to step into God's kingdom plans and providing support for them while they do so.

Does your ministry take teens seriously as kingdom workers now? Where are the places young people are being given real influence? Consider how you might equip teens to lead worship, preach, plan events, and take ownership of evangelism and discipleship strategies. Honoring teenagers goes beyond honoring their gifts and what they can do for the ministry. Honoring teenagers also includes valuing their opinions, their connections to the Holy Spirit, and taking seriously how they challenge the local church's status quo. Strive to create a youth ministry where teenagers feel and are shown that they are honored and taken seriously.

A CULTURE OF RELATIONAL HEALTH

Finally, biblical culture values relational health. In Acts 2, Scripture shares how the early believers worshiped together, ate together, and provided for one another. The believers practiced humility and valued one another above themselves. A youth ministry that values humility will be led by youth workers who understand people are a little messy sometimes, so we need to do all we can to keep relationships healthy amid the messiness of life.

Conflict is bound to come up when we do life with one another. Youth workers need to make their youth ministries spaces where it is common to ask for forgiveness from others when we mess up and where we extend forgiveness to others when they hurt us. Forgiveness and conflict resolution should regularly be subjects of sermons and discussions. Youth ministries may also benefit from youth workers who can mediate tense conversations. Leaders should not ignore difficult situations but model how to handle them well for the sake of health in the community.

Finally, what would it look like for teenagers to know that your youth ministry is a place where their needs will be met and where they know they are welcome to help meet the needs of others? Highlighting stories of God's provision through believers is one method of cultivating this culture. Additionally, consider creating ways for teenagers to share their needs with one another, whether material or spiritual.

A CULTURE WORTH CULTIVATING

The culture of your youth ministry impacts the effectiveness of your evangelism and discipleship efforts. Therefore, youth workers must step back from time to time to get an accurate reading of the culture of the ministry. Ask hard questions. Take the opinions of teenagers seriously. To benefit your teenagers, youth ministry, and the kingdom of God, take steps to cultivate a culture of belonging, honor, and relational health in your ministry.

THINK PRAYER

by Zach Coffin

I KNOW I DON'T HAVE to convince you that prayer is essential. If you are reading this book, you have probably preached a few sermons on the topic. So, let me ask you a question: What if prayer was not just an "add-on" to your ministry but rather the fuel that powers your ministry? What if prayer becomes the primary ministry of your ministry?

Prayer has been the foundation for every great move of God. In the hills of Kentucky in 1801, over 8,000 Conestoga wagons carrying roughly 20,000 people gathered to pray. This prayer meeting was the largest of its kind and served as the primary spark for the Second Great Awakening in the United States. One hundred years later, in 1903, a young man named Evan Roberts heard a sermon where the pastor prayed, "Lord, bend me." That simple prayer wrecked Roberts and sparked the great Welsh Revival that saw more than 100,000 come to salvation because of an encounter through prayer. In southern Indiana, I met a lady named Roberta. Roberta was in her eighties and understood the power of prayer. She dedicated the last years of her life to be at youth camp every summer. Every time the students were on the campus for camp, you would find Roberta praying in the sanctuary and finding students to pray over. Roberta would teach the teens that prayer was their greatest weapon for life's many trials. Prayer has always fueled the fire of the Holy Spirit's movement.

Sadly, prayer has been watered down in many ministries. It has become a few short words we say before meals, before we take a road trip, and something we do in a service to get our students to be quiet. Prayer has lost its power in our youth ministries, and it's time we rekindle the fire that has fueled every great revival.

If we cognitively know that prayer is the power source for our ministry, why do we overlook its significance? I believe it's because we simply don't prioritize what matters most. We all live in the tension of "one more thing to do," but it's time we trade good things for the most important thing.

This trade happened for me in 2016. Our ministry was growing, and students were being saved and baptized. From the outside, we were a flourishing ministry. The problem was that the ministry felt manufactured and not empowered. We had great programs, but God's presence was not moving in power. I began to seek the Lord for clarity as to why I felt this tension so deeply. I quickly realized that prayer was part of our ministry, but not what we relied upon. Prayer was a reaction to needs rather than the source of our strength. After this realization, I started a prayer meeting after youth group; our youth group was never the same. We began meeting for one hour after our regular youth group to pray and worship, and I saw our students grow more deeply during that time than any programmatic strategy.

Here are four key ways our students grew as they prayed.

1. Students learned that God is approachable.

In today's culture, students feel desperately alone, and prayer is the antidote to that loneliness. As the students learned to pray, they saw that God was near and approachable. They began to see his love and wanted to speak with him. They discovered that God was very present and near, whether they were at church, in their room, or in the hallway. God was no longer a distant fantasy but became a close friend they talked with whenever they needed him.

2. Students learned God's voice.

As the students prayed, they discovered what the voice of the Holy Spirit sounded like. No longer did they solely rely on our ministries, sermons, or small groups to be the voice of God in their lives. They begin to walk boldly because they heard God speaking to them.

3. Students learned where true power comes from.

I watched as passive students became passionate about Jesus. Our youth ministry was fun, attractive, and reached students across the county, but as they learned to pray, students began wanting more of God and less programming. I watched as boldness, courage, and strength grew exponentially. They no longer wavered in their commitment to God, and as God answered their prayers, their faith grew deeper. They began to realize that it was not our ministries' clever ideas that were drawing people but rather the Holy Spirit's whisper.

4. Students grew hungrier for the things of God.

Hunger for God was the most significant fruit of their prayers. I watched as students began reading their Bibles, worshiping, sharing Jesus with their friends, and even laying hands on each other and believing God for miracles and healings. We even saw healings take place before our eyes. Praying to God grew hunger for God.

As students learn to pray, they need help from you and your team, and they need words, models, and creative ways to articulate their prayers. Below are ten simple ideas to help cultivate prayer in the lives of your students.

TEN WAYS TO CULTIVATE PRAYER IN YOUR YOUTH MINISTRY

1. Cultivate prayer in your own life.

If you don't love to pray, your students won't either. We often struggle to model prayer because it's not a part of who we are. Ask the Holy Spirit to teach you how to love prayer.

2. Start small.

Find two to four students who will commit to pray with you for thirty minutes before or after the service. Don't over-program the time with teaching on prayer—just pray.

3. Pray during service.

I'm not talking about a fifteen-second prayer before the message. I'm talking about taking ten to fifteen-minute blocks during your service that you provide for students to pray over and for each other. Have them break into groups. Have them pray into the microphone. Teach them how to pray in silence without technology. Use your youth group time for more than just preaching and music. Allow prayer to become a programmed, intentional decision.

4. Repeat after me.

I was recently preaching at a camp in Maryland when one of the pastors, Pastor Brent, invited the students to pray after him. I'm not talking about the salvation prayer. He would pray with passion and enthusiasm, and it gave the students language for their prayers. This simple practice helped give students words to pray, and hearing the roar of the room praying together was truly a joyful noise to the Lord.

5. Pray Scriptures.

Teach students to find Scriptures that relate to their circumstances and pray those words. I commonly hear students say, "I don't know what to say." By teaching them to pray the Scriptures, we are not only arming them with language but God's heart for their lives.

6. Find a tool that works for you.

There are a thousand prayer tools on the internet to help teach students to pray. Choose one and use it for an entire school year. Don't teach a new tool every week. Teach one and stick with it. Use it in your services. Model it in your small groups. Have students pray it from the platform. Find a tool and use it.

7. Teach students to lay hands on each other.

Okay . . . I know it's youth ministry, and you instantly think about the gross couple in the back. Don't let the gross couple keep you from teaching James 5. When we teach students to pray for healing, by using James chapter 5 as a model, we stretch their faith and build a love for each other as they petition God. James 5 provides a great model for teaching prayer over each other.

8. Ask how You can pray for the student right now.

This is a question I always ask my students and volunteers whenever I meet with them. They are not going to leave my presence without me praying over them. I do this in formal and informal settings, and I want to normalize that friends pray over each other regardless of location or time. This practice keeps prayer as the central piece of all we do; over time, your leaders will begin to model the same practice.

9. Host prayer meetings.

I believe it's time for the prayer meeting to make a serious comeback. Every great revival can be traced back to a prayer meeting, and it seems to be a consistent theme for any mighty move of God. What would it look like for you to build prayer meetings into your normal youth group schedule?

10. Spend time with people who pray.

You just had a few people come to your mind. You know who these people are. They are people that have the spiritual gift of intercession. I promise the more you hang out with them, the more prayer will grow in your life. Invite them to your youth group and take your students to their prayer times. The more we are around prayer, the more it will grow in our lives.

Out of the list above, try to pick three ideas to try in the coming months. Teaching students to pray will teach them how to speak to God, and most importantly, it will help them recognize his voice. Prayer has been the fuel for revival generation after generation. What if God wanted to use your students' prayers to spark the next great awakening? I believe he does.

THINK SOCIAL MEDIA

by Paula Rae

SOCIAL MEDIA CAN BE A tremendous platform for ministry. Nearly every parent and student in your community is on at least one social platform. If used well, these platforms can help you reach people connected to your ministry as we ll as many more who may never cross the threshold of your church building. But you could easily miss the opportunity to build connections and even share the gospel if you see social media as a promotional tool rather than a ministry tool.

The primary thing to remember about social media is that it is a social platform, so be relational on whatever platforms you choose for connecting with your students, parents, and the community. If you were meeting someone in person, you would never spend the whole time talking about yourself—the person you're meeting would roll their eyes and walk away! Instead, you would ask them questions about themselves or comment about something you think you might have in common to start a conversation. It's a similar dynamic on social media. Say something entertaining or tell a funny story. Ask engaging questions. Share words of encouragement. Give a shout-out to volunteers or a local business that is doing something great for the community. Ask how you can pray for people, encouraging them to reach out either in the post comments or in a direct message. Limit posts that promote upcoming events to one for every five relational posts.

Social media—when used correctly and efficiently—can help you build relationships and minister to people. But, for all the potential opportunities social media offers to churches and student ministries, it has some pitfalls that leaders must be mindful of as well. Here are some important and practical things to consider as you establish policies and develop plans for using social media.

WHO IS SEEING IT?

While social media can be used as a tool, it's important not to be ignorant about the people on the internet and the dangers that exist online. When considering social media, it's imperative not to accidentally expose personal information. Being private about addresses (if it is someone's home) and students' identities could potentially save lives. A good tip to follow is when posting about events that are hosted at someone's home, have people "DM" or text you for the address. (It's okay to talk about it at church, however, especially if you have public social media accounts; not everybody should have access to personal addresses.)

Public accounts can be great for reaching students through the internet. If your youth is reposting things on their stories, then their friends are seeing the fun things your youth group is up to, and it will get your foot in the door. But you should be actively checking for followers that seem suspicious. This isn't being judgmental; it's being safe. On your end of "following," a good rule of thumb is to only follow students that you have actively seen at your youth group. You should not treat the account as your personal one; do not follow your friends, celebrities, etc.

LIABILITY AND LEGAL (PHOTOS, FOSTER CARE, ETC.)

You need to have an awareness of those in your youth group who, for legal reasons, cannot be posted on social media. Students who are in foster care cannot under any circumstance be put on the internet where their identities might be exposed. So, be hyperaware. Most students are okay with being posted, but it's always a good idea to check with students before posting.

WHO IS RUNNING IT?

This can vary, depending on what you are willing to do and want to do. Running an active and effective social media account is more work than it seems, so make sure that you—as a youth pastor, leader, etc.—don't bite off more than you can chew. Those who run the social media account/accounts should always be an adult within the youth group. This person should know the ins and outs of social media, not someone who has never used it before. While students—especially student leaders—might have the desire to run the social media account, it's probably best to have an adult run it.

WHAT IS POSTED?

Youth ministry social media accounts can be used for anything from daily encouragement, youth ministry announcements, church events, or even funny, Christian content. You can be as active as you wish, but it's important to at least have a presence on social media. Through platforms such as Instagram or Tiktok, you or your volunteers can post things that will be encouraging to your students throughout the day. You can pull from your sermon series or just post about Scripture that is speaking to you. Youth are led by example; if they see you in the Word, they'll be more likely to be in the Word themselves.

IS IT BEING USED EFFECTIVELY?

"Selling" your ministry should not be your goal. However, with the power of social media, you can show the followers, especially those who might be "unchurched," that church can be fun and exciting. (There is a stigma around social media that causes people to believe that it can only be evil, useless, or pointless. However, with the increasingly technological world, social media can be used to benefit your youth group. Students who come across your page should be able to see the youth ministries' mission, purpose, and culture. It should be obvious what and who you are all about.

YOUR PERSONAL SOCIAL MEDIA

Your life and personality should be consistent in each aspect of your life. If the person you portray on social media is different from who you are in reality, you need to check yourself. Being an effective minister means not being hypocritical. One of the main reasons people do not attend church or even like Christians is because they find so much hypocrisy within the church. Especially when dealing with youth who are impressionable and watching every little thing that you do, being the same on and off social media is important for your character and your influence. It doesn't matter how old you are, if you as a youth pastor are posting a night out drinking, the students will think that's okay. And the list goes on. Be consistent; be holy.

YOUR VOLUNTEERS' SOCIAL MEDIA

The standard for your volunteers' social media should be the same as yours as a pastor. Your volunteers need to be accountable to the people so that what they project on social media is consistent with who they are as followers of Christ.

It's also important for leaders not to engage with students too much over social media to protect both parties. There shouldn't be texting about things unrelated to the ministry between people of opposite genders. Leaders should not have deep conversations with students over text; set up a time in a public place. Leaders should not be posting about yet-to-be announced activities without the permission of the pastor first. Leaders shouldn't post private prayer requests either; what is shared confidentially needs to remain confidential. Leaders should also allow for students to reach out first and follow first. Don't seek your students out on social media; allow them to do that. Something specific, but important, is that there should be no Snapchat communication between leaders and students. Any social media form of disappearing pictures is a terrible idea for both the student and leader. Safety comes before anything.

MOST EFFECTIVE PLATFORMS

For students, the most effective social media platforms in 2023 are Instagram and TikTok. Most students are on these platforms, so they are more likely to see and be invested in the youth ministry social media account. Instagram and TikTok are also built around account growth, so if the goal of your social media is to get the word out about your youth ministry, then these have the most effective algorithm to grow and get the word out.

SOCIAL MEDIA FOR STUDENT LEADERS

If your youth ministry has a leadership team, then your student leadership should also be conscious of what they're posting on social media. When they enter the student leadership team, students should sign a contract to represent the youth ministry—and Jesus—well. Student leaders are often the most influential students in the group; therefore, their lives on social media should also be consistent with who they are in real life.

SOCIAL MEDIA AND PARENTS

Parents are more likely to be active on Facebook, so having a Facebook page to minister to them as parents and share announcements is a good idea. Parents are curious; they want to see what their children are involved in or could potentially get involved in. Your posts for parents could assure them of ways you are looking out for their kids' safety, update them on biblical themes you're teaching, or even share parenting ideas and encouragement. The teen years are challenging for parents, too! Again, the goal isn't to promote the youth ministry; it's simply to build relationships and minister to people in a positive and exciting way.

THINGS TO CONSIDER

Finally, brothers, whatever is true, whatever is honorable,
whatever is just, whatever is pure, whatever is lovely,
whatever is commendable, if there is any excellence, if there
is anything worthy of praise, think about these things.
—Philippians 4:8 ESV

- Social media posts must reflect the values of the ministry and the church.
- Your pastor must have the ability to ask for deletion of a post.

CODE OF CONDUCT FOR CONTACT

- Adults should not Snapchat with minors.
- Social media: Wait for minor to follow first. → Leader must contact supervisor if they are contacting a minor individually and then recap (with discretion) what the conversation was about.
- Social media communication must only be used for the purposes of spiritual growth of the student and for relationship with the volunteer that cannot be done well face to face or in the group chat.

WHEN PROBLEMS ARISE

- If the situation upholds biblical standards and the esteem of the student in communication, but does not follow policy:
  - 1st offense: personal meeting with supervisor
  - 2nd offense: removal of influence on said student(s)
  - 3rd offense: immediate removal from the ministry
- If the situation does not uphold biblical standards or violates the esteem of the student, the consequence is immediate removal from the ministry.

- What is considered "major" and "minor" is up to the discretion of the supervisor.

PARENTAL CONSENT FORM

- Parents must provide consent for volunteers/staff to communicate with their child electronically through social media accounts, group chats, and personal messaging.
- Parents must also consent for their child's picture or name to be utilized in social media.
- Communication and/or photo and name utilization cannot be done until the form is signed.

THINK CALENDAR

by Charlie Alcock

"THINK CALENDAR" IS ANOTHER TOOL of the ministry toolbox. To *think calendar* means to be aware and alert of specific dates, events, holidays, etc., that occur on a daily, weekly, monthly, or annual basis. Crafting a calendar that takes into consideration what is happening in the local school(s), the local community, and the church will bless your ministry. Failing to consider all of these could sabotage your ministry.

When done right, you are helping people see the future and open doors for people to be active and involved in your ministry.

How important is it to *think calendar*? Will thinking about the calendar truly affect the way ministry happens through and around me? Does an awareness of the calendar make any difference at all in my life or my students' life?

The answer is yes! It is important and it will affect your ministry, your life, and especially your student's lives.

Go into event brainstorming with a specific thought and mindset. Events should be planned with this mindset: "If a student only comes tonight, what impression will they have of our ministry?" Asking such a question creates consistent ministry experiences.

Below is an outline of a master calendar:

SCHOOL YEAR

August—Kick-Off Bonfire

September—Worship night

September—See You at the Pole location

October—Fall Fest

November—State Park Retreat

November—Missions Meeting

December—Christmas Party/ Dinner

January—New Year's All Nighter

January—Worship Night

February—SOUPer Bowl Party

February—Love the Community Event

March—Blacklight Dodgeball

March—Youth Retreat

April—Culture Carnival

May—Senior Sunday Send off

SUMMER

June—Summer Spectacular

July—Youth Camp

Looking at this outline, we are able to note both specific and broad events, dates, holidays, etc., that happen throughout the year. This aligns well with the biblical strategy and is a tool that can be used to better help ministry.

THINK FAMILIES

by Amanda Drury

LAST SUMMER, I GATHERED SEVEN families together for a planning retreat to dream up ways in which the church might support parents and caregivers. Every family had some kind of expertise in ministry related to young people. At the start of the retreat, we asked participants to answer the following question: "When I think about passing on my faith to my kids, I feel…" By far, the two most popular responses were "overwhelmed" and "anxious," with "hopeful" coming in a distant third. We were struck by these responses, especially in light of the fact that all of the parents and caregivers had some kind of professional experience with the spiritual formation of young people. I was struck by the thought: If family faith formation is so difficult for the experts, how much more intimidating must it be for the average parent?[1]

There tends to be a high level of anxiety amongst parents and caregivers concerning the topic of passing on their faith. With that said, however, study after study shows that the religious lives of young people are largely dependent on their parents. What you see in the parent tends to get passed on to the teen. If you have a teenager who is able to talk about their faith, chances are they have a parent who is just as, if not more, articulate.

A teenager's homelife tends to be more spiritually formative (or deformative) than anything that takes place at church. That's not meant to discredit the amazing ministry that takes place in churches or camps, it's simply an acknowledgement that a teenager spends way more time at home than they do school. In their book, *Handing Down the Faith*, Christian Smith and Amy Adamcyzk sum it up this way: the key people to pass along faith are parents. The key location is the home, and the key methods are regular, ordinary, everyday practices.[2] Families matter.

But we've got a problem. Families are tired. They are overwhelmed. They are busy. Smith and Adamcyzk write: "Religion, no matter how important parents consider it, is often not as important as other priorities, especially sports and homework."[3] There are tangible, immediate consequences to skipping homework or blowing off a soccer game. The consequences of skipping church aren't as readily seen. This is an uphill battle. And yet, we believe that the Holy Spirit works in and through both the church and home to cultivate a life of faith for teenagers.

And so, with that said, let's look at two places where youth workers can help cultivate family discipleship with teenagers.

INTENTIONALITY

We all know that parents and caregivers are important in passing on their faith to their children. Recent research has pointed us towards one of the major factors that contributes to children actually wanting the faith of their parents—the *warmth* of the parent.[4] Parents who enjoy a warm relationship with their children tend to have an easier time passing on their faith. That probably seems pretty obvious. *Of course, a father is going to have a difficult time passing on his faith to his kids if he's cold and withdrawn.* What would it look like for a youth group to intentionally invest in the parent/teen relationship? Are there events that the church could host that would bring the two together?

In my first youth ministry job, we hosted a "bridge" event every semester. Twice a year, we would open up the youth group for parents to attend. Instead of breaking into small groups, teens would talk with whatever adult came with them (we had adult leaders available to meet with the teens without a parent or caregiver). We did very little teaching on these nights; the majority of the time was spent facilitating conversations between a parent/guardian and their teen. A dad might not be likely to share his testimony with his son on a random Tuesday, but if he's explicitly asked to do so in a church gathering, it is far more likely to happen. Over and over again we heard teenagers say things like: "I had no idea that happened to my mom." Or, "I've never heard my dad tell that story before." And the teenagers who were often tight-lipped at home had a set-apart space where they were prompted to open up with their parent/guardian. It was simple, but intentional, and it was perhaps my favorite part about being a youth pastor.

EARLY INVESTMENT

Churches that are large enough to support a youth pastor likely have someone running their children's ministry as well. There tends to be a line between Sunday school and youth group. What might it look like for you to partner with the children's director to find formative ways to teach parents how to teach their kids from the youngest age possible? In my early ministry days, I kept coming back to the same thought: "I wish I could have gotten to these teenagers when they were younger. I wish my ministry included some kind of ministry to parents/guardians of young kids, because if the adults could model what everyday faith looks like when their kids are little, that would have a huge payoff in youth group later on." It's easier to learn a language when you are young (in this case, a language of faith). Even though it might seem out of "your area," see where and how you might support families with young kids. Work with other leaders in your church to determine how you might encourage spiritually formative experiences in the home beginning at birth. What are the milestones a parent/guardian might celebrate and how might the church help infuse those milestones with faith? Is your church providing the kind of care and encouragement to young families that would prompt you to be at the top of their list to call when they're in crisis?

Statistically speaking, faith formation tends to have the greatest impact within the home. When you look at the typical week you spend as a youth leader, you likely have time set aside for preparing lessons or meeting with teenagers. Perhaps you are planning and organizing an upcoming event. Part of building up the faith of teenagers means investing some of your time in finding creative ways to get families to engage with one another. Because families matter.

[1] Note: I've been using the phrase "parents and caregivers" in recognition that families are a lot more complicated than a teenager living with a mom and a dad; with that said, for the remainder of this chapter, when I say *parents*, I am including *caregivers* as well. Caregivers is meant to include grandparents, other family members, foster parents, etc. This is particularly helpful to remember when you are creating permission slips for teenagers. Using broader language sends the signal to the teenager that it doesn't matter who they live with, there's a place at church for them.

[2] *Handing Down the Faith*, Christian Smith and Amy Adamcyzk, p. 70.

[3] Ibid., 28.

[4] Ibid., 5.

THINK COMMUNICATION

by Amber Cook

IT IS ACCEPTED AS FACT that one of the most destructive traits in a marriage is poor communication. In fact, poor communication is often referred to as one of the top causes for divorce (along with financial stress and unfaithfulness). Many times (though not always), financial stress and unfaithfulness are secondary issues that stem in some way from poor communication. For pastors who journey with couples through premarital counseling, communication skills are always on the list of emphasized topics. If a couple can learn how to communicate well, they are highly more likely to have a lifelong, fulfilling marriage. So, it is with communication in student ministry.

POOR COMMUNICATION KILLS MINISTRIES

One can't help but wonder how often poor communication is behind youth ministry leaders parting ways with their churches. **The truth is that poor communication kills ministries, while healthy communication enables ministries to flourish.** As a leader in student ministry, developing robust communication tactics must be high on your priority list.

What sort of communication tactics do you already have in place? How do you communicate what is happening in the ministry? How do families know what events and programming are available? What sort of patterns do you have in place for communicating?

LEARN COMMUNICATION METHODS

In premarital counseling, couples are often asked to engage with material from Gary Chapman's book *The 5 Love Languages: The Secret to Love That Lasts.* In this book, Chapman proposes that different people give and receive love in such different ways that they can be classified as different languages. For example, some people receive love best through words of affirmation while others receive love best through acts of service. The point of the book is to encourage people to know their own love language as well as the love languages of their spouse, children, friends, etc. According to Chapman's philosophy, people often attempt to communicate their love to others in ways the recipient doesn't understand. This, then, creates a disconnect in the relationship.

In a similar way, there is a plethora of communication methods available to your student ministry. You could be communicating in every way from verbal announcements to billboards to social media to letters to texts to notice boards to phone calls to videos to emails to table tents to informational meetings to fliers to everything in between and many more! One of the first steps you can take toward "think communication" is brainstorming all the different communication methods you could be using as a student ministry. **What options for communication methods are available to you?** (Be as "blue sky" in this brainstorm as possible. Don't limit yourself to options you've used or options you prefer; maybe even include "homing pigeons" and "singing telegrams" to remind yourself the sky is the limit! The goal here is to come up with as comprehensive a list as possible. Actually, take some time to grab a pen and paper to make this list as you will need it later.) How familiar are you with those options? What sort of training or resources would you need in order to utilize different communication methods? What methods are you or someone in your ministry very familiar with? Are you leveraging those methods well? What methods would you like to be able to add to your communication toolbox?

KNOW YOUR AUDIENCE

If a wife learned about the five love languages and discovered her own, yet failed to learn the love language of her husband, the exercise wouldn't prove very helpful for the strength of their marriage. However, often those of us in student ministry leadership can be guilty of finding communication methods that suit our preferences without considering if they are received well by our intended audience. For example, if I rely on Facebook to communicate with parents and guardians of the students in our ministry when over a third of the parents don't have Facebook accounts, I'm going to get into some trouble. I could be the most thorough communicator ever on Facebook while still totally failing to communicate with over 33 percent of my intended audience.

Part of the challenge student ministry leaders face is the sheer number of audiences we need to communicate with on a regular basis. It would be easy to focus exclusively on communication with youth. As a youth ministry leader, this is likely (though not necessarily) a stronger skill set for you. However, the most fruitful student ministry leaders understand they actually have at least ten target communication audiences. Yes, you read that correctly. **As a student ministry leader, you have at least TEN different target audiences for communication.** Some of these audience categories could easily be broken down into smaller groups, but ten is an easier number to work with initially. You will notice that each of the ten listed below is given a letter code. As you read the description of each group, pull out your brainstormed list of possible communication methods. Jot that group code by each method you think could be helpful in communicating with that group. (If you want to split the groups down smaller or add to them and create your own system, go for it! These ten target audience categories are just to get you started.) Along with communication methods, you also must consider communication frequency as part of your communication tactics. How often does this particular audience need to "hear" from you?

1. Y: YOUTH IN THE CHURCH

How can you best communicate with the youth who are already engaged in some way with your church? This group could easily divide down further into smaller groups. For example, there may be students who are part of your Sunday morning worship gathering but not connected to your midweek student ministry; there also may be those who are engaged in some form of student leadership. Consider those who are just completing their time in your church's kids' ministry—how do you best communicate with them? When should this communication begin?

2. PC: PARENTS OF YOUTH IN THE CHURCH

Parents are likely to receive communication best in ways quite different from their teenage children. What kinds of information will they need from you, and what are the best ways to get it to them? Again, this group could be subdivided. There are likely parents of teenagers in your church who have yet to support/encourage their children to engage in student ministry programs. What kind of communication might those parents require? How about parents who are new to the church themselves? What does communication look like with parents who don't attend your church while their teenage children do?

3. V: VOLUNTEERS IN THE STUDENT MINISTRY

One of the best ways to lose volunteers is to not communicate well with them about expectations, vision, time commitments, schedules, etc. How do your volunteers want you to communicate? What communication methods are the least stressful for them as people volunteering their time? Again, you are likely to have volunteers in different capacities that may require different communication tactics. What do van drivers need to know and how? What about chaperones? Small group leaders? You may need to create a database of the different categories of regular volunteers in your ministry in order to think through the different communication tactics required.

4. SP: SENIOR PASTOR

As a student ministry leader, you want to be 100 percent confident that your senior pastor is as fully in the loop as they want to be on everything happening in the student ministry. As a general rule, you want your senior pastor to be the first to know things. The pastor needs to be able to have your back in any given situation, so you never want them to be surprised by anything. How does your senior pastor prefer you to communicate? What is too much communication versus not enough? Develop a clear communication tactic for this very important audience.

5. OS: OTHER STAFF AT THE CHURCH

Remember that as a student ministry leader, you are part of a larger team with all the ministry leaders/staff at your local church. This larger team needs to be a prioritized communication audience as well. You often will be sharing common spaces for ministry events as well as putting schedule requests on the same families. For example, if families in your church have children in both the kids' ministry and the student ministry, you want to ensure that the programming for both are not creating any form of tension or conflict with each other. What needs to be communicated with other staff members, how, and how often?

6. B: BOARD OF ADMINISTRATION/ELDER BOARD

Depending on the leadership structure of your church, the "board" could have a different name, or there could actually be more than one board that requires your communication. This body is often one of the most influential in the church alongside the senior pastor and staff. Don't forget to communicate well with them! Does this board expect a written report from you as student ministry leader? A verbal report? How often?

7. WC: WIDER CHURCH CONGREGATION

Even members and attendees of your church who aren't directly connected in any way with your student ministry should have access to certain information about the youth ministry. How will you give them this access? What do you want them to know? How do you best communicate with the whole church?

8. CL: COMMUNITY LEADERS/ORGANIZATIONS

Who are those key leaders in your community who are outside your church but would be great partners or resources for your student ministry? What about community organizations such as schools and not-for-profits? Develop some tailored communication tactics for these leaders and organizations. Begin to build or enhance relationships that could be incredibly fruitful for the kingdom in the future. What communication methods would work best for these leaders and organizations?

9. CY: COMMUNITY YOUTH

As a student ministry leader, how could you begin to communicate about your student ministry with teenagers in the community who aren't yet connected to your ministry in any way?

10. CP: COMMUNITY PARENTS

Many families who are unchurched would be curious about programs available for their teenagers. How could you communicate with unchurched parents about opportunities available to their young people through your student ministry?

THINK PROTOCOLS

by Carsyn Stout

ASK "WHAT IF...?"

Working with children has taught me to be prepared to answer a variety of questions. I could be in the middle of a lesson about Abraham and Isaac, and a student will yell out "Um . . . could you please explain the Trinity to us? I really don't understand that." Of course, I want to jump on the opportunity for learning, but these questions often lead us into a spiral of more questions. This is how I felt when I was addressing the idea of implementing protocols within my children's ministry. It seemed as if I could write forever about policy and protocol for how we should handle different situations. I was drowning in possibilities on what to cover, but I felt stuck all at the same time. That is when I asked the "what if" question. This question drove my motivation and outline for creating my volunteer handbook: the book that outlines our policy on a variety of situations that could occur within my ministry.

ANSWERING THE "WHAT IF...!"

There are a few basic policies that you should have within your handbook. These include the natural disasters that could occur in your context. What if there is a fire? How do volunteers exit the buildings? How do you verify with each adult that all students are accounted for? By beginning with the "what if" question, you can have more focused questions follow. Do not let your mind go too far into the what if. It is vital that you write your policy in a way that covers a range of situations with common solutions. Designate a point person who oversees answering questions or dealing with situations when you are unavailable.

This allows your volunteers to know the plan, if you're not there to take point. You can design policies that provide more outlined situations for you and those you select to help. By answering the "what if" questions, you can cover the situations that may occur within your ministry.

CONTEXT IS KEY

This quote can be overused, but it remains true. The context of your ministry is key to guiding how you address what policies you need. Your questions are also driven by your context. You must identify the needs of your context prior to implementing protocols. Not only is the city you are located in important in determining how you evaluate your context, but the church or organization you are working with determines your context. Evaluate your students and their families within your environment. How would they best benefit from and be protected by the policies you are implementing? Once you identify this, you are able to write effective protocols for your ministry.

ASK FOR HELP

When beginning policy writing, do not do it alone. Your church elders, coworkers, and volunteers are great resources to bring into the conversation. Meet with a variety of people within your context to work through the difficulty of policy writing. The more brains that are present, the more well-rounded your protocols will be. It is important to get things in place before it is too late. The guilt of those who feel stuck in situations where they do not know what to do is a hard guilt to live with. I know this from personal experience, but also from witnessing others when there is an uncertain situation. You as the leader in your church or organization hold the weight of making sure your volunteers are equipped to handle a variety of situations that could occur within their time in your ministry. Equip them! There is training focused on developing policy for volunteers available. Utilize these resources to the best of your ability. The more people who know the plan—the policies and the protocols—the better! Protocols should be in place to protect everyone for any future situation that might develop.

THINK ROOM DESIGN

by Rev. Amber J. (Livermore) Cook

HAVE YOU EVER ATTEMPTED TO go on a date hoping to have a deep, meaningful conversation, only to discover that the place you chose to go isn't conducive for this AT ALL?! Maybe the music is way too loud, the seats are far too uncomfortable, or the room is so crowded that you feel like five other people are listening to everything you have to say? In the same way, students will come to your student ministry looking for a place to hear from Jesus, build deep community, have fun, and feel safe. Don't let them leave without those experiences because of poor room design.

SPACE MATTERS—IT EVEN SPEAKS!

The layout of your ministry space matters. There must be intentionality in choosing a ministry space as well as in designing it. When I took my first job as a youth director in a small church of less than a hundred people, the youth would meet in a corner of the church fellowship hall on a few old couches that someone had donated. The youth ministry name was printed out on a few sheets of yellowing printer paper and hung above the couches on the bland white fellowship hall walls. Don't get me wrong, there were advantages to those couches! I've seen worse ones for sure, and they were comfortable! (I took more than one nap on them when I was stuck waiting at the church between services or meetings!) However, that space was speaking things I didn't want to communicate. Your ministry space has something to say as well—have you listened to what it is telling your students?

Every other age group in the first church where I served had their own ministry room except for the youth. This spoke volumes to the students about their lack of importance, even though I'm convinced no one in the church ever actually thought of them as being less important. Not only that, but the space was far too public for real or deep conversations—at any moment, other people could walk through the fellowship hall. This was distracting, and it told the students this was an unsafe space for vulnerability. The student ministry name above the couches, while perhaps important to a previous generation of students, was no longer relevant to the teenagers who were gathering with me on those couches. It also looked dilapidated and forgotten. In addition, the rest of the fellowship hall was filled with tables and chairs that were used regularly in different ministries, so it was difficult to expand our youth area on days more students arrived than usual. Finally, the couches encouraged a level of closeness between couples who were dating in the youth group—a closeness I preferred to avoid!

A ministry space should be an asset to ministry rather than a hindrance to it. Take some time to evaluate your current ministry space—look for any aspects of the space that might be distracting from or even standing in the way of your ministry strategy. Remember that space matters, and you can make adjustments so that work a FOR kingdom purposes rather than against them.

NO EXCUSES—IT'S WORTH IT

Some churches are blessed with significant facilities and generous budgets for room design. What a gift that is! Even so, most ministries have to choose to prioritize how they will invest their finances in ministry. We often aren't able to afford to do all the things in ministry we dream of doing. It would be easy for any ministry to neglect room design for the sake of other worthwhile investments in activities, events, mission trips, curriculum, food supplies, etc. However, no matter the size of your budget, there is no excuse to not think strategically about your room design. Churches with lots of resources and churches with minimal resources can always find ways to invest in their ministry spaces—and they should because it's worth it!

Let's go back to that youth corner with its couches. My small church had a very minimal youth budget, and our building didn't have any stellar alternative options with a neon sign that said "THE PERFECT STUDENT MINISTRY ROOM!" However, I knew that something needed to change. The church did have an old choir room. Have you ever seen those in churches before? It had a massive closet across one whole wall for hanging choir robes. The room was intended so that choir members could robe up before heading out to the sanctuary platform. Our church hadn't utilized a choir ministry in years (and I doubt that even if it had been resurrected, anyone would have wanted to wear robes!). The room had turned into a meeting room for the church board with a massive table filling the whole space other than the empty choir robe closet. I approached the church board to ask if they would surrender their meeting space so the youth could utilize this room as their own space. After all, the church board met when no one else was in the building—so they could easily use the fellowship hall or an adult classroom for this. When I presented my case to the church board, they wholeheartedly agreed. This began our quest to turn an old choir room into a student ministry room.

When I started the process of shifting the youth space to the old choir room, I also started taking a Youth Programming and Management class with Charlie [author]. The first day of class, he explained that part of our grade would be a project called "Monster Church" where we—as a class—would renovate the student ministry space of a local church. I already knew I had my work cut out for me to renovate our ministry space on a next-to-zero-dollars budget, so I approached Charlie privately after class asking if I could be exempt from the project in light of the project I'd already taken on myself. To my delight, Charlie's response was, "Well, what if the class takes Monster Church to your church?" I was stunned. This opened the door for more ideas, more creative resourcing, and heaps more energy and manpower!

When Charlie brought our ministry need before the class, everyone was asked to start considering their different connections to possible resources. That semester, our class was able to acquire materials for a stage, a screen, a projector, speakers, and tall coffeehouse-style tables and stools. The cost to the church was minimal compared to the value of the items. We raided the attic of my church and discovered old wooden chairs—the kind that were so old that they had somehow become cool while collecting dust. We took a sledgehammer to the old choir robe closet (I got to inflict the first blows ☺) to expand the room size and make room for the stage. The connections and work of my classmates transformed our next-to-zero-dollars-budget project into a pretty amazing room makeover!

What excuses might have prevented your student ministry in the past from investing in room design? Do you believe it's worth it to prioritize what your ministry space is saying? What kinds of conversations need to happen within your church leadership structure to begin to change the status quo of your room design? In what ways might you be able to gain creative access to different resources in order to make your room design an even better asset to your ministry strategy? Who could you reach out to for ideas and resources?

ROOM DESIGN IMPACTS OWNERSHIP

Intentional design of a ministry space gives students the chance to own that space as well as the ministry that takes place there. Leading up to the Monster Church youth room renovation, I started journeying with my students through a process of discerning a ministry identity that they could own. We looked at who we were called to be biblically as a student ministry. We brainstormed about how we wanted our student ministry to be known in the community. We came up with a few different ministry names, prayed over those names, and eventually voted on one. (I was disappointed at the time that they didn't pick my favorite; looking back, their pick was WAY better than mine!)

After we took out the choir closet, our students and regular volunteers spent an evening painting the new, but still empty, room. Rather than the bland white walls of the fellowship hall, this room would have some color. (Let's be honest, after the students left that night, my volunteers and I stayed late repainting everything they had painted! However, it was so important that they were part of the room design process.) Once the paint dried, the team of college students in the Youth Programming and Management class came in to install all the equipment and bring in all the furniture. The room makeover was complete!

I will never forget the next youth group night when we let the students come into their new space for the first time. Their eyes were huge, and their faces were covered with smiles. Their new student ministry identity was projected onto the screen. They found seats around the tall tables at the back or on the vintage wooden chairs near the stage. The energy in the room was something our student ministry had never experienced before that night!

The best part of a room design that promotes ownership in students is how it begins to amplify ministry strategy. After that night, something incredible started happening. Students were excited about the ministry and began talking about it at school. They started bringing their friends to youth group. New commitments were made to Christ. Teenagers were growing in their faith. Suddenly, young people in our church were owning their part in the ministry strategy because they owned their ministry space and identity.

What level of ownership do students have of the ministry in your church? How does this correlate with the priority given to their student ministry space? Have students been able to contribute to the room design in any way? How could they be given more ownership of their student ministry space?

UPDATING IS A CONSTANT NEED

There's nothing more frustrating than jumping on a church's website, trying to find information about their programs, only to discover that it hasn't been updated in years. In a similar way, ministry room designs require constant updating. The couch corner I found when I arrived at my first church was at one point a very intentional room design. It likely served a great purpose for a season, but by the time I arrived, it was in need of an update. The last time I visited that church again, do you know what I discovered? Our stage was gone. The walls had been repainted in very different colors. The furniture we had used—gone. Everything looked different—and that is a GOOD thing!

Sometimes we can have so much ownership over spaces we helped design that we forget that no room design is meant to be permanent. When was the last time your student ministry space got a face-lift? Maybe it is still functioning well, but some minor changes need to be made to keep it current. Brainstorm ideas of what updates are needed over the next six months.

TIPS FOR USING SHARED SPACES AND TRANSFORMING SPACES FOR SPECIAL EVENTS

I served for four years as the national youth consultant for the Wesleyan Methodist Church of Aotearoa–New Zealand. The focus of my role was supporting student ministries and their leaders in our churches around the nation. The Wesleyan Methodist Church there was fairly young at the time, and only a few of our local churches owned their own buildings. Most of our churches rented community spaces for their weekly ministry programs, and even those who did own a building often had lots of ministries operating out of the same spaces. Clearly, in contexts like these it simply isn't feasible to renovate a room specifically for student ministry. I was so impressed as I observed our student ministry leaders in New Zealand who had developed creative ways to design rooms (even without a permanently designated space) that supported their ministry strategy. If you find yourself using a shared space for your student ministry, you can still find creative ways to design your room week after week. This takes a level of work, but it also inherently provides opportunities for uniquely designing your space for the specific activities planned for each week. These same principles are useful for rearranging a space for a special event that needs to feel "different" from weekly youth group meetings.

First, one of the easiest ways you can shape your room design is through how you set up your seating. Most ministries taking place in shared spaces are not confined to permanent seats like pews. Usually you can totally change the feel of the room through how many chairs you set up, how those chairs are oriented to the rest of the room, and in what formation the chairs are placed. You always want enough seating so that students don't feel crowded (i.e., room to grow), but you also want to limit the number of chairs so that the room has the energy of being "full." One of our churches in New Zealand had volunteers show up every week about an hour before youth group to take down about 150 chairs in the sanctuary and reorient the remaining chairs at the front near the stage for youth group. This became a marker for the students that the space was "theirs" rather than the whole church's for that night. The open space at the back, then, became a space for games and activities. Of course, this also meant that volunteers and students had to reset the space after youth group for other ministries.

Second, lighting can easily transform a space into a different feel. This can be accomplished through adjusting stage lighting or dimming lights. You can even use lamp lighting to give a softer, living room feel while turning off ceiling tube lights. Changing the lighting changes the space and can create a sense of ownership.

Third, stable but mobile furniture or equipment can be used to as a divider to set apart a shared space to a specific room design. The same student ministry I described that reset chairs every week before and after youth group also transformed a food serving area into a snack shop every week. The importance of the snack shop had less to do with making any money than it did about creating an environment. Students could walk by the same countertop on a Sunday morning before congregational worship and not even notice it, but on youth group nights, that counter became a place for socializing. Another student ministry had different sets of equipment for games and activities that would be set up in the same spaces every week in their shared space. This accomplished the same purpose!

If your student ministry has to operate out of a shared space, what sorts of tactics do you use to still prioritize room design? What additional design elements could you include to support your ministry strategy?

SANCTIFIED SPACE

I have always admired "Umfundusi" Jim Lo for his emphasis on sanctified space. Any time "Umfundisi" is going to minister in a space or is aware of others who will be ministering there, he takes the time to ensure that the space is set aside for ministry purposes. A couple years ago, "Umfundisi" came to preach at my church. He arrived much earlier than "necessary" and began to prayer walk through the church building. He anointed every entrance with oil and prayed over every seat in the sanctuary. This is a perfect example of sanctified space.

Not only is a space set apart through prayer and the welcoming of God's presence, it is also set apart by keeping evil presences and influences out of the room. This includes practicing spiritual warfare prayer to force any unclean spirits to leave. It also means keeping clear protocols in place on any activities, videos, music, etc., that will be used in the room, so that no unclean spirits are unintentionally allowed into a space set aside for ministry. Of course, as an example, this doesn't mean you can't have a fun movie night in the student ministry room, but it does mean that you and your team are careful about what movies are shown.

No matter how perfect your room design might be, ultimately it is the welcoming of the Holy Spirit in the room that will enable your ministry strategy to produce real kingdom fruit. When was the last time someone prayed over the seats in your student ministry room? What blessings have you prayed over the entrances and exits, covering everyone who will come in and out those doors in protective prayer? Have you ever anointed ministry equipment with oil, setting it apart for only God's use and purposes? Do you have guidelines in place to protect your ministry space from activities that might work against your ministry strategy? Ensure that your room design is a sanctified one!

THINK VOLUNTEERS

by Nate Kingsbury and Pricilla Youn

YOUTH MINISTRY IS ESSENTIAL TO the Christian community. The youth are the leaders for the generations today and for the years to come. Because of that, we must continue investing in the lives of our students, to better develop and disciple them through youth ministry. One way to do so is through volunteerism. According to Merriam-Webster, volunteerism is "the act or practice of doing volunteer work in community service." In the context of youth ministry, volunteerism is the act or practice of doing volunteer work in student ministries.

One of the greatest reasons we need to think volunteers is based on the encouragement and command we receive in 1 Peter 4:10: "Each of you should use whatever gift you have received to serve others, as faithful stewards of God's grace in its various forms." Thinking volunteers pushes us to envision what it looks like to use the gifts that God has given us to better serve his kingdom. In other words, considering the importance of volunteers allows us to provide room and roles to be filled by those God has equipped and gifted.

To better understand this command, one must understand what it means to volunteer, how to recruit volunteers, and why one should volunteer.

WHAT DOES IT MEAN TO VOLUNTEER?

Volunteering is not only doing "good" for the community, as we often think of it to be. Volunteering is one way to express gratitude and faith to Christ. Volunteering is serving his people and his kingdom, which also testifies to who Jesus is and whom we are all called to reflect.

In Ephesians 2:10, we are reminded of how and why we are crafted: "We are his workmanship, created in Christ Jesus for good works, which

God prepared beforehand, that we should walk in them" (ESV). We can approach volunteering—understanding it to be a good work—with confidence, knowing that God has prepared the way for us.

Finally, understand that to volunteer is to teach. Volunteering teaches compassion, self-sacrifice, wisdom, and guidance. Volunteering in a youth ministry context gives youth the opportunity to work through real challenges and make meaningful change.

WHY VOLUNTEER?

Volunteering Provides Purpose

The Lord calls each person to serve, naming it a good deed
and how that brings glory to his name.
—Matthew 5:16

Serving through volunteering gives one the opportunity to live into his or her purpose as God prepares the way. A deeper sense of purpose is exemplified as the volunteer becomes a part of something greater than him- or herself.

Volunteering Provides Community

Volunteering can help one feel connected to those they are serving in the community. It provides ways to be a part of a community and be present in that community.

Volunteering allows one to pour into a community and the community to pour back into the volunteer.

Volunteering Provides New Relationships

Volunteering is a great way to meet new friends and continue friendships with pre-existing friendships. When one volunteers, that person is exposed to new relationships that can be made and easily pursued. Volunteering is also a great way to continue friendships that were once made in the past.

Volunteering allows relationships with students as well. Specifically, in the youth ministry realm, volunteers are given opportunities to connect with youth through events, activities, and conversations, and creates a space to build those relationship. Common interests are oftentimes found between volunteers and youth students in these contexts.

Volunteering Provides Valuable Skills

When one volunteers, they are placed in an environment where old and new skills can be discovered. These skills include interpersonal communication, time management, leadership, delegation, problem solving, relatability, and inclusivity.

Volunteers can grow in each of the skills listed above and apply those skills in different parts of life as well.

Volunteering Provides FUN

Volunteering is fun. Volunteering gives so much life. When one volunteers, that person engages in fun activities and growth. It's fun and exciting to be around youth students and explore one's interests and passions while doing so. Youth ministry volunteers are placed where they can share joy and laugh with students, which is always a plus!

In the midst of finding volunteers, teaching how to volunteer, and practicing volunteering yourself, remind yourself of the core reason to do this particularly for youth ministries: to serve the kingdom of God.

HOW DO YOU RECRUIT PEOPLE WHO WILL BE LEADERS IN MINISTRY WITH YOU?

Look to see how potential volunteers interact with people. Look to see if they can have fun and laugh. Look for leaders that can help offset your weaknesses; we all have them. Look for leaders who deeply care for people.

1. If you see the gifts in a person, go to them and engage in conversation.

- Get over your fears.

- Remember people want to be needed.

- Have fun when recruiting.

- Be you when you recruit.

    Side note: You have to develop your own voice for recruiting leaders. Don't be afraid of rejection; 80 to 90 percent of people I ask say no, but 10 to 20 percent say yes.

2. Don't sound desperate when recruiting. For example:

- "I need leaders!"

- "No one wants to help me!"

- "We have been shutting down classrooms."

- "You don't serve anywhere in the church; you should help me."

3. The best recruiting is word of mouth.

- New recruits are open to help if the leader of the ministry is willing to ask them.

- Flyers, announcements, and upfront plugs from the pastor may get a few, but don't underestimate the power of a personal contact.

- Ninety percent of people recruited are from my personal interactions.

4. Recruit with Vision

> *I charge you, in the sight of God and Christ Jesus and the elect angels, to keep these instructions without partiality, and to do nothing out of favoritism.*
> *—1 Timothy 5:21*

- Give them the big picture.
- Get them excited.
- Let them realize they can make a difference. Example: I am the pastor at Stoney Church. Our mission is to "love God and love

people." How do we do this? By teaching people to know, grow, and go in the power and love of Jesus Christ.

- Love God—love people.
- Realize you have the ability to help people grow and you are not afraid to go.

5. Define clear expectations with a detailed job description.

- Be clear about what you are asking of them.
- Don't assume they can read your mind.
- Put something in their hands.

6. Make time to recruit.

- Plan time to recruit, despite busy schedule.
- Look for new recruits constantly.
- Attend key leadership events.
- Block out time on your Outlook calendar for recruiting:
- o Use Sunday morning before and after church for recruiting.
- o Greet parents as they pick up their students.
- o Use ministry events.
- o Use leadership events.

7. Develop a pool of new contacts.

- Ask your existing leaders to give you names.
- Ask key leaders of your church. (Remember leaders know leaders.)
- Ask pastors on staff.
- Check out the college ministry in your church and campus ministries.
- Look through contacts that previously served.

8. Always take notes.

- Walk the lobby.
- Use your surroundings.

- Notice people in natural settings.
- Keep a record of new leader contacts.

9. Create entry points to serve.

- Start with responsibilities where they excel.
- Give them time to grow into a role.

Remember: Throwing people into the deep end of the pool is not teaching them to swim; it's poor leadership on your part.

10. Love on your leaders.

- Send them an e-mail the day they volunteer.
- Give them a personal call the next day.
- Value their effort.
- Celebrate them in public.

MORE TIPS

- Don't be intimated if a leader is more gifted then you; understand the impact you will achieve together.
- Always give ministry away. Volunteers will do certain things way better than you.
- If a leader does not seem like a fit for a certain role you are looking for, create another role for them where they are gifted
- Look at the commitment and discipline of the new recruit. Do they turn in the forms on time? Do they call you back when you call?
- Don't be afraid to recruit a new Christian who is a mature person. I believe serving is one of the best discipleship processes.
- What is the best recruiting plan? The one you chose to actually use?

THE HARD PART IS VOLUNTEER EVALUATION

What to Evaluate

The "what" of volunteer evaluation is completely rooted in the expectations that we have for a specific ministry volunteer. Job descriptions are specific to each ministry volunteer and are rooted in the overall mission and vision of the ministry.

When to Evaluate

Evaluations should take place at various times of the year, depending on the specific ministry calendar. The ministry leader should give and receive feedback in an informal manner, while sometimes having surveys or forms.

Who Evaluates?

Each evaluation should include at least two people evaluating to allow for self-discovery of gifts, concerns, and success. Allow a leadership team to speak into those areas as well.

Volunteer Evaluation Forms

Design a form that everyone on your team uses. This helps you hear from them and learn things about how you can lead better as well.

Warning!

Conflict will happen, it's inevitable. It's how you handle conflict that makes the deference in your leadership. There are entire books on conflict management. Go find one and read it.

THINK SCHOOLS

by Geoff Eckart

THE SCHOOL CAMPUS IS THE most strategic mission field in America. Think about it: there is a school campus in every community in our country. Your community has one. Every community has one. Geographically and sociologically, it's a hub that connects the overwhelming majority of our society. If you want to influence not only the present but the future, you cannot overlook the role of the school campus.

Consider this:

- Over 95 percent of our population goes through the portal of middle school and high school.
- Students spend over 50 percent of their waking hours on a school campus during the academic year.
- The average student will spend over 9,000 hours on a school campus during their middle and high school years.

Where else is there a place and space where practically everyone in that society will be physically gathered together and there is a location in each and every single community within that society? There is only one: the school campus.

There is tremendous opportunity for kingdom impact when we think of our local school. Jesus' words in Matthew 9:35–38 accurately describe this:

Jesus went through all the towns and villages, teaching in their synagogues, proclaiming the good news of the kingdom and healing every disease and sickness. When he saw the crowds, he had compassion on them, because they were harassed and helpless, like sheep without a shepherd. Then he said to his disciples, "The harvest is plentiful but the workers are few. Ask the Lord of the harvest, therefore, to send out workers into his harvest field."

Jesus went to all the towns and villages in this community. Rather than waiting around in synagogues and the temple for people to come to him, he went where the people were. Jesus met them on their turf. He took the time and effort to go where they socialized, worked, and lived their lives. He was strategic in everything he did, and these few words in Matthew speak volumes about Jesus' strategy.

The same should be true for you: you must go where the people are. If you wait for students to come to you, realize that many of them never will. Regardless of how great your ministry is, or how amazing your church facility might be, the open door for them to attend your ministry will be the one that you open when YOU go to THEM. If you are working with students, the clear front-runner for going where students are is their school. Maybe you can physically be there on a campus, and maybe you can't. But there are ways of "going to a campus" without physically being there. Remember, Christian students will always be able to be on campus, and they are the true missionaries. The reminder is to be equipping them to reach this strategic mission field.

Jesus had compassion on the crowds. He saw them for the people they were—those that mattered to God. Matthew gives us insight into Jesus' heart when he tells us that Jesus observed that the people were harassed and helpless. They needed someone to look out for them, but no one was. He looked beyond their faults and facades and saw the highest potential in them, as well as the fact that they were image bearers of God himself. He didn't blame them for being lost; he loved them. His spirit was deeply moved as he looked at the people before him. It went beyond emotion to action. He felt for them but also reached out to them.

Nothing replaces true compassion. When God grips your heart for people, it will shake the very foundation of your soul. Nothing can stop the person who is filled with the supernatural compassion of God. It's easy to look at people and see things that distract and dissuade us from having the same perspective that Jesus had. Don't get caught up in seeing the surface and fail to look beyond it to the deepest parts of someone's soul. Everyone needs the love of God, and once this love for another takes ahold of your heart it is an unstoppable kingdom force that will bring a person from spiritual death to life.

Schools are ready for harvest. Unfortunately, Jesus' assessment that the workers are few is still true in many respects. As a ministry leader, you have to ask yourself this critical question: Will I be a worker in this ripe and ready harvest field?

THINK CONTEXT

by Rev. Amber J. (Livermore) Cook

IF YOU'VE EVER MADE A global or cross-country move during your lifetime, you will know from experience that different contexts are just that—different. Culture, geography, history, socioeconomics—all of these factors have an impact on how people see and do life. This is certainly true for young people as well, though it is actually often even more complex when it pertains to students. Youth culture has a way of creating its own unique perspective on life even within a broader cultural context. As someone in student ministry, you must learn to "think context." The tactics you use to accomplish your ministry strategy need to adjust according to the context or even be dictated by the context of your ministry.

1. LISTEN FIRST

As a missionary in a foreign (to me) country, "listen" had to become a sort of mantra for me. The best way to "think context" is to learn to listen well. Any time we are new to a context, our greatest danger is that we will not hear the experiences, cultures, needs, and concerns of the people to whom we are called to minister. It is too easy to assume that those around us see life through the same lens we do and not really hear them when they tell us otherwise. One of the most important passages of Scripture to the people of Israel and to the Christian church is found in Deuteronomy 6:4–5, which reads, "Hear, O Israel, the LORD our God, the LORD is one. Love the LORD your God with all your heart and with all your soul and with all your strength." The Hebrew language understood something about "hearing" that might require a lesson for many of us. For the Hebrew, to hear did not simply mean an auditory process that enabled your brain to register sounds; rather, to truly hear something would be evidenced through the appropriate responsive action. In other words, hearing was actually listening in order to respond. In the case of hearing God, of course, this would mean listening to obey. In the case of hearing the people in a ministry context, this means listening in order to learn for the sake of discerning fruitful ministry tactics.

One of my earliest student ministry contexts was in a very low socio-economic setting. I found that one of the best ways I could engage with students was through offering to take them out for a meal, ice cream, or coffee. This was highly appreciated, and the gesture itself often opened the door for deep, real conversations that provided perfect opportunities for Jesus encounters. In my next student ministry context, I was ready to jump right back in with this same tactic. However, I began to notice that things were very different. These students came from rather affluent families. Often when I would take them out, they would offer to pay for my meal. The "event" of going out for a treat was not all that meaningful for them, and the conversation often didn't go much past surface level. Eventually, I discovered different ministry tactics that were much more meaningful in that context, such as organizing community service together in our area. I had to listen to the context in order to find tactics that worked.

How often do you take time to listen to your context? How do you structure your ministry life to hear the needs and concerns of your students and their families?

2. LEARN IN ORDER TO TEACH

We are meant to be lifelong learners, and we always can learn from others, even those we are called to teach. The most effective teachers are those who are committed to being learners of their students. It's only when you learn how students process situations and learn what is of most interest and concern to them that you can then present information to them in the most life-changing ways. Therefore, to be a great teacher in a student ministry context requires a posture of humility to learn from your students. Of course, you as a youth pastor or ministry leader have knowledge and experience that needs to be passed on to your students. This is a given. However, they also have knowledge and experience of their own context that you need in order to package well what you have to offer.

One simple tactic you can try in this area is through "surveying" your students. You need to learn the best way to do this—whether through an actual written or electronic survey, large group discussion, one-on-one conversations, or a series of small group meetings. Let your students know that you want to learn about them—challenges they're facing in life; questions they have, whether about life in general or Christian faith specifically; areas of curiosity or interest for them; etc. Let your students know that what you learn from them will impact your tactics in ministry during that season. Allow them to speak into some of the topics for your preaching/teaching curriculum. Go to them to find out what days/times make the most sense for weekly youth ministry programming and ministry events. Encourage them to share their ideas with you for how the ministry can reach more students.

I grew up in the Midwest where almost every youth ministry met on Wednesday nights. At the time, society was so culturally impacted by this pattern that most sports teams never had practices or games on Wednesdays because it was "church night." Plus, it just made sense that students would get church exposure on Sundays with the wider congregation with Wednesday providing a mid-week discipleship opportunity. I was shocked while living in New Zealand that Wednesday was NOT youth group night for the majority of our churches. It took me a while to sort out the reasons, which were many and legitimate, but student ministry was typically a Friday night activity! In my hometown context, Friday would have been a terrible night to try to get students to come to youth group; in Auckland, it was the best night possible for most churches! If I hadn't been willing to listen to learn first, I would have been trying to steer our student ministry leaders in a wrong direction based on my ignorance of the context.

The most significant learning you'll be able to do is learning through relationships. Take appropriate opportunities to "do life" with your students and the families of your church/community. Learn about their families, cultures, backgrounds, and worldviews.

Consider inviting some specific individuals to help you learn the context; give them permission to draw your attention to any of your oversights. As you learn, ask the Holy Spirit to show you how your new understanding should shape your ministry tactics. You'll be amazed by how far a learner's posture of humility will take you in the process of teaching students about following Jesus.

What are you currently learning from your own context? What is God revealing to you about the needs in your community? How can you more intentionally begin to learn from your students and their families? Ask the Holy Spirit to reveal ways you've assumed things about your context without taking the time to learn.

3. EMBRACE INCARNATION AND STUDENT MINISTRY

When Jesus came in human form to earth, he "incarnated" himself among us. He left his home in heaven, came in the flesh, and lived among us. He came to us and did life with us in order to reach us. If you're going to "think context" for your student ministry, there's no better way than following the example of Jesus. Jesus humbled himself and joined us in our mess (though without sin) in order to bring us salvation. Student ministers are most effective when they practice a similar form of incarnational ministry.

Incarnational ministry can be difficult and messy, and it is certainly time consuming. Being truly incarnational means finding ways to do regular life with students. It means leaving the office to spend time on a school campus, sacrificing free evenings to attend student activities like sporting events, musicals, or art shows, and accepting invitations to meals or birthday parties. Incarnation could mean substitute teaching or volunteering at your local school. It could mean coaching a team or chaperoning a dance. The more you can engage with students in their normal lives, the more you are following Jesus' example in going to them in order to reach them.

When we engage with students where they are, we communicate that they matter. The effort to be part of their lives outside of student ministry pays great dividends in what we can learn about their context. We can actually listen to our students' lives rather than only what they can articulate about their lives. Incarnation is the ultimate posture of humility, and it allows us to listen and learn best.

Part of incarnation is adapting our own culture to fit best in our context. This can be tricky as an adult youth worker. No one (including students) expects you in every way to act and dress like a teenager. However, there are certain aspects of cultural context that will require your adaptation. For example, language learning is always a priority for cross-cultural missionaries. While you may not need to learn a foreign language in your context, there are elements of language that vary from one context to another even within a language group. Sometimes you may have to laugh at yourself with students as you "learn their language," but this is part of being incarnational. Another example would be methods of communication. If your preferred communication method is Facebook when none of your students use it, you're going to have to learn an appropriate way to communicate that suits your context. Dress is also an area that may require your adaptation. Again, even your students might be appalled if you tried to dress like THEM, but there are certainly ways of dressing that might be off-putting in a given context.

Consider your average week in student ministry: what percentage of your ministry time is spent incarnationally rather than in your church context? Are you satisfied with that percentage? What would it take to intentionally increase the amount of time you spend doing life with students? How might you need to adapt your own life patterns in order to better connect with your context?

4. LEVERAGE YOUR FAILURES

Even when you're trying to listen and learn as you incarnate yourself in a local context, you will inevitably get it wrong sometimes. When you fail to listen well to a context, you are given two great opportunities. First, you have the opportunity to learn. We often learn more from our failures than from our successes. Second, you have the opportunity to demonstrate true humility by being able to own your mistake and even laugh at yourself. When we show true humility in how we respond to our own contextualization failures, it will often earn a lot of grace and respect from those to whom we are ministering.

As an overseas missionary, I have more contextualization failure stories than you would ever want to hear. One that was particularly humiliating took place on a women's retreat. I was part of the spiritual leadership team for the retreat. For the last night, everyone was divided into groups to present some sort of a fun "act." I ended up taking the helm for organizing our leadership team to present a silly rap song about the retreat. During one of the group times for brainstorming and practice, one of the participants on the retreat started teasing me, asking if our leadership team's presentation would be any good. Everyone was listening in, and I responded emphatically, "Oh, we're pros!" The atmosphere of the room immediately became awkward. One of the other retreat leaders finally spoke up, "Pastor Amber, I'm not sure what 'pros' means in America, but here it means 'prostitutes.'" I was mortified! I'd just called all the spiritual leaders in the room prostitutes! I explained that I had intended to call our retreat leaders "professionals." Then we all had a hearty laugh about the whole thing!

Believe me when I say I learned a lot from that contextualization failure about not assuming any sort of shortened words or slang meant the same thing in my current context as my home context. Not only did I learn, however, but I also practiced laughing at myself. As you might imagine, that moment came up a few (or many) times after that—"Remember when Pastor Amber called all the female pastors prostitutes?!" Rather than responding defensively, I owned the mistake. I even told on myself to others and initiated the laughter. This was an amazing opportunity to connect with people on a human level, and it opened doors to deeper ministry relationships.

Okay, here's one more failure story I will share. My first Easter as a missionary was spent with a large group of Pacific Islanders at an Easter youth camp. I was asked to preach for Easter Sunday morning, and I was very aware that I didn't own any truly culturally appropriate clothing for the occasion. I had a few wrap skirts, but they were far too casual for Easter Sunday. I asked a Fijian female friend if she would help me dress more appropriately. She brought me a dressy sulu—a wrap skirt with an elastic waistline made of silky material—that I could wear under one of my shorter American dresses. I was so excited that this wrap skirt couldn't fall down like my casual ones that required tucking or tying. I dressed for service and proceeded to preach my heart out. Through the whole sermon, however, I noticed the old ladies in the back snickering and giggling. I couldn't figure it out! Was something I was saying not communicating properly?

After the service, I approached the old ladies at the back. I was determined to figure out what I had missed! One of them spoke up immediately, "Great sermon, Talatala!" (Talatala means "Pastor" in Fijian.) She then added, "Just maybe next time, don't wear your sulu backwards so you can walk easier!" All the old ladies cracked up laughing! Sure enough, in my familiarity with a skirt that had an elastic waist, I had missed that it was still important to have the bottom open portion of the wrap at the front. I had been taking baby steps the whole time I preached because of the restrictive nature of wearing the skirt backwards!

Just like the misspeak moment I described earlier, this wardrobe malfunction became both a learning moment and an opportunity to respond with humility to my own error. I told this story in pretty much every Pacific Island context I ministered in after that day. I laughed at myself with students who thought my contextualization fail was hilarious. This opened the door for deeper relationships and deeper ministry opportunities.

You don't have to leave the country to change contexts. Even moving to a church on the opposite side of town can come with subtle differences that may prove important to your ministry tactics. Don't be afraid to learn about your failures due to ignorance of the context. Invite trusted people who have been part of the church or community longer than you to point out contextual or cultural matters you may overlook. It's true that as a ministry leader, you can begin to shift and shape the ministry context in many ways, but you'll want to be aware as much as possible if that is what you're doing. The awareness that you're calling for a shift will help you understand and respond appropriately to any friction caused by the changes.

How do you respond when you realize you missed the mark in understanding your context? Do you leverage your failures for learning and demonstrating humility? If you are in a relatively new context, who are some people like my fellow retreat leader or row of old ladies who would be willing to kindly call you out when you get it wrong? Have you invited people to correct your contextualization errors?

5. FIND NEW WAYS TO LISTEN AND LEARN

Don't stop listening and learning! Sometimes people who have lived in one context for a long time only see it as it was a long time ago! It's easy to miss what is changing right in front of you, or at least to not be intentionally conscious about changes and what that should mean for your ministry tactics. There's a reason dying churches are known for their last words: "We've always done it this way." In most cases, their tactics at one point were spot-on for what was needed for their context. Their tactics were effective ways of working their ministry strategy. However, at some point along the way, those churches chose to stop listening to and learning from their contexts. They didn't notice when certain programs would have been more effective if offered at a different time. They weren't aware how the top needs in their community had shifted. They were ignorant of the disconnect in their communication methods. Don't become so comfortable in your context that you stop listening and learning!

Ask yourself: How could your student ministry structure itself for continual listening and learning? What kinds of annual or even quarterly practices should you adopt for staying current with your understanding of your community?

THINK TEACHING & PREACHING

by Mark Schnell

IS TEACHING AND PREACHING TO youth still a valid expression of youth ministry today? Sure, teaching and preaching are still the norm in adult church; it's kind of expected there. What about doing this for teens though? Is this method of ministry outmoded in a culture that is so used to brief TikTok videos and countless other types of social and digital media? Don't teens have attention spans that are too short for an extended sermon or Bible lesson? The answer to all these questions is a firm no! We've seen God use preaching and teaching to great effect today. The Holy Spirit regularly transforms the lives of teens through preaching and teaching that is centered on the Word of God and contextually focused on students and their experiences. God still uses this powerful form of ministry today, and what's more, it can be as effective as it's ever been in history. Let's look at a few key components of effective preaching and teaching to youth. We'll start first with you as the preacher/teacher and then speak to the message and method.

CONFIDENCE, CALLING, AND AUTHENTICITY

Almost everyone who has stood in front of teens to speak has at some point had the thought, "I can't relate to these kids; I've got nothing to connect with them about." Some people feel this so strongly they give up, never to try it again. Others, sadly, might go down the rabbit hole of obsessing over how to become cool enough to connect. I have a secret to share related to being cool enough to connect with teens: The moment you aged out of your teen years a kind of separation was built between you and them. This does not mean for a second that you can't or shouldn't try to connect and relate to them at a deep level. It does not mean that you shouldn't try to know their culture, especially how to understand the vernacular of the day. These are all important things that should be given proper attention, but the separation I mention only means that you are not one of them. There's good news—teens don't need you to be one of them. Whether they realize it or not, they don't need you to dress like one of them or to try to speak the way they do. These things usually end poorly anyway because we try too hard. What they need is the unique perspective God has given you about his Word and how to live as a Christian. They need to hear about your successes and failures and the grace of God at work in your life. If you've been called by God and by a church or ministry to teach and preach the Bible, then do so with the confidence that can only come from the Holy Spirit. You've been placed in that important position of spiritual authority and responsibility. Live into it!

Authenticity is another important aspect related to calling and confidence. Be your authentic self when you relate to youth. Whether you're in your twenties, your seventies, or anywhere in between, be yourself. Lean into your age and enjoy that. If you try to use a teen saying and mess it up, laugh at yourself. Be in on the joke. They'll laugh with you and the pressure will be off. You should never make yourself the hero of every story—God should hold that role—but don't be afraid to speak of your failures and how God taught you, or how his grace covered you. On the other hand, don't make the mistake of going too far with self-disclosure. When in doubt about how much to share about your own experiences, seek counsel from someone with more experience than you, like a lead pastor or another spiritual leader. The important thing is, if you've been called to teach and preach to teens, rely on the One who has called you. Be confident about being who you are, at whatever age, and be your authentic self.

BE WINSOME

Winsome is a word we don't often use much in our culture today, but it's a fitting one related to preaching and teaching, especially to teens. It simply means to win people over, to be cheerful and engaging. A winsome person is the one who others are happy to see, who adds value to people, and makes them feel they belong. Your teaching and preaching should be winsome. One of the main reasons is that your source material, the Bible and the Christian life, are the best news the world could ever hear. You should be a winsome teacher and preacher because many of the teens you speak to (1) do not have anyone in their corner cheering them on and making them feel welcome; and/or (2), in the midst of the raging hormones and social anxiety that goes along with being a teen today, they simply feel out of place or a bit odd. The winsome youth speaker reminds them they aren't odd, and they do belong.

When you speak, whether in large groups or small ones, interact directly with them. If a student interrupts you with a question or comment, don't get annoyed, just interact with them. Related to this, ask questions of them, and then allow them room to talk. Don't act surprised when given the kind of answer that only a thirteen-year-old boy or girl can come up with. If you teach or preach using curriculum, make sure to get beyond what is written on the page and apply it to those specific teens in that specific time and place. If you're a camp speaker or Bible teacher, engage with the campers. Don't just show up five minutes before you speak, but hang out with them, play games with them, sit next to them in meals. The same applies to local church ministry. Get to know them the best you can. The best preachers and teachers are winsome and concentrate on making meaningful connections with students before, during, and after delivering a lesson or sermon.

BE BIBLICAL AND DEEP, BUT CONNECT

TED Talk and motivational speakers, stand-up comedians, and preachers all speak in public before an audience. The first three have their place and can be beneficial and enjoyable for listeners, but they differ from preachers in one key aspect: preachers communicate God's love. Communicating God's love as found in the Bible is the most important facet of your role as a teacher or preacher. After all, you are sharing the very message of life with them.

One mistake preachers and teachers make is underestimating what teens can handle. They fear that teens will be overwhelmed with too much depth in sermons or lessons and the result is teaching and preaching that has more in common with cotton candy than the spiritual milk and meat that all followers of Christ require for growth. At the same time, though, it is possible to go too deep, to make your sermons and lessons more like lectures than conversations where students are interacting with you and the Word. Here are a few things to consider in this area:

1. **Preach and teach the Bible.**

   Do studies on books of the Bible or do lessons and sermons on things the lead preacher or preaching team are presenting, focusing on application in students' lives. Use curriculum as a guide to help you find biblical studies to concentrate on. Connect with other youth ministries, sharing ideas and insights with others on the what and the how of preaching and teaching the Bible.

2. **Without biblical content your teaching and preaching may be no more than pop psychology and entertainment.**

   Those things have their place but remember your role and calling as a minister.

3. **Don't confuse your teaching and preaching with entertainment, but work hard against boredom.**

   It's been said that it's a sin to bore people with the Bible. If this is true, it's especially so with teens. Use lively stories, metaphors, and illustrations that students can relate to. Don't be afraid to use humor and interact with your students as you ask questions and encourage discussion. Another good rule of thumb related to boredom in preaching and teaching is, if you're bored with what you are saying, they are even more so. If students are bored with biblical teaching and preaching, you're probably doing it wrong.

4. **Speak with passion.**

   Allow the Word of God to impact your own life before you communicate it to others. You won't be able to teach it any other way than passionately.

5. **Depth is good but preach and teach for appropriate lengths.**

   You should try and keep sermons closer to twenty minutes than forty. The longer you preach and teach the better you must be and the greater the chance that you will overwhelm your listeners with more than they can apply to their lives.

6. **Stick to one primary Scripture rather than jumping around with many different texts.**

   Using supplemental texts to support the main one can be useful, but only as they serve the theme of the main text. Using too many texts confuses people. Think of your sermon or lesson as going on a journey with your listeners instead of winning a court case by piling on proof-texts or more points than they can ever follow.

7. **Don't beat them over the head with things they have to do to become "better" Christians.**

   Look for what God is doing in or behind the text and how God's grace empowers us to live the Christian life.

8. **Think of the sermon as a chain of linking items.**

   Link each movement of the message with the one that comes before. This helps with short attention spans and wandering attention, both for the listener—and even you as the speaker.

9. **Remember, you can only do this work because the Holy Spirit makes it possible.**

   You are never alone in this; God wants to bless your work and to communicate his love through you. God has chosen you for this amazing task.

10. **Bathe every part of the sermon or lesson in prayer.**

    Have others praying before, during, and after everyone.

THINK LIFETIME

by Andrew Morell

I'M A PASTOR WHO LEADS a church in the community where I grew up. This community has a history of great high school basketball, and I have a court for the community to play ball right next to my house. It's just one piece of my life and ministry that reflects something about the city I live in and care about. There is more, much more. It's about people and simply loving people—all kinds—from all walks of life and ages. Maybe my ministry today was in some ways influenced by people who loved and cared for me when I was young.

There is one story that is a good example of how your ministry to someone today can result in a connection with a person for a lifetime. It was in middle school that I met this youth pastor. I was not easy on him, and my friends were not either. We all knew he liked us, and we used that to our advantage. When he took us home after youth group meetings, we always ended up at a 7-Eleven® getting drinks and snacks. One time, we snuck in the back door of the bus headed to see the Cincinnati Reds™ baseball game. When he discovered us, he didn't send us home; instead, he bought us tickets. My journey with this youth pastor had begun and the stories would only get better. Youth group nights, youth camps, retreats, parties, and basketball leagues were all part of this season of life. The impact he made in my life was something I wouldn't understand until years later.

Then he moved away, and I lived my life my way. During the rest of my high school years and after, I did things that would lead me down a road that would nearly take my life. I remember the night a guy stuck a gun in the window of my truck and pulled the trigger. My face bled profusely as I sped away in hopes of finding a hospital. The first words that the doctor said to me were, "Young man, I don't know how close you are to God, but you are a destined man." There was no way that I should have been alive. I knew it was God and I needed to change.

Let me tell you this, God's word does not return void (see Isa. 55:11). God's word from all those people who spoke truth into me, including that youth pastor, were words that God brought back to me during this crazy time of need in my life.

After my recovery, I was sitting in a Starbucks™ that had just opened up in my town. It was a warm summer night in July. I had my Bible open, and that place was slammed with people, with no open tables or chairs. The door opened, and I saw this youth pastor; it had been seven years. He walked right toward me, and I got up and walked right toward him. We didn't care who was in that Starbucks™ or who saw us; we hugged and, yes, even cried.

This relationship that was forged years ago when I was in middle school was rekindled that night in July, and today it's a friendship that runs deep. There are days when he comes to my office asking for prayer and advice. There are days I come to his office asking for prayer and advice. There are days when we just go out to that Starbucks™, get a coffee, and talk about how God has given us some amazing stories and sweet memories that are pushing us to make new ones and build toward the future. He now serves on my Sanctuary Team as we prepare to design a new ministry space for the seven-year-old church plant that I founded.

So, what is the secret to our relationship, and why has it become one that has lasted this long? It's Jesus. Our bond is that our relationship is based on our common pursuit of Jesus, proclaiming his name and loving his people.

Here are a few things to think about:

- **Think eternal.** Remember that you may never see the results you desire in a student's life, but that doesn't mean you've failed. Like I said earlier, God's word doesn't return void.
- **Think developmental.** It simply takes time. Rome wasn't built in a day, and neither is a lifelong relationship.
- **Think little steps.** Be ok with little wins along the way. We want to see leaps and bounds, however, it's the little steps that, when you look back, move a relationship down the road.

CONCLUSION

I MET DARREN THROUGH A mutual friend. Darren led the youth ministry at one of the largest churches in the country. I drove up to Chicago to meet with him not knowing how if this would be a one-time meeting or the beginning of a lifelong friendship. It turned out to be a great few days, and I invited Darren to speak to a group of youth pastors at a leadership conference. I will never forget the Friday night of this conference when he challenged us all and said "the extraordinary things that you desire for God to do in your ministry, begin with everyday ordinary acts of obedience." After he finished speaking, the room, filled with pastors, including me, were on their knees committing to do the everyday ordinary things that God has called us to. The things that nobody ever sees. The things that make you get up early in the morning. The things that keep you grounded. The things that reveal your discipline and desire to be faithful to the One who has called you.

I want to encourage you to see and value the everyday ordinary things that Jesus did as a example for us, knowing that it is Jesus that can do the extraordinary through us and the ministry we lead. I also want you to dream. Dream about the extraordinary, the moments that everything you have been praying for happens. I encourage to keep dreaming and believing that what God has called you to is to see the extraordinary in the lives of ordinary people. It's not that we must choose between the everyday ordinary and the extraordinary, it's that we understand their relationship.

Finally, my hope is that you will embrace the biblical truths that shape us a disciple and shape our ministries in making disciples. When we are grounded biblically, the process of discovering God's plan and direction for our ministry becomes a labor of love. That's what we all want! We all want to know and feel the eternal purpose that fuels the passion of our labor. And we can!